Training Youth for Dynamic Leadership

Training Youth for Dynamic Leadership

Loveland, Colorado

Credits
Contributing Authors: Tim Baker, Bob Buller, Karen Dockrey, Karl Leuthauser, Tom C. Long, Erin McKay, Todd Outcalt, Janis Sampson, Pamela J. Shoup, Trevor Simpson, Dave Thornton
Editor: Amy Simpson
Creative Development Editor: Dave Thornton
Chief Creative Officer: Joani Schultz
Copy Editors: Helen Turnbull and Debbie Gowensmith
Art Director: Ray Tollison
Cover Art Director: Jeff A. Storm
Cover Designer: Fuller Creative Inc.
Cover Photo: Digital Stock
Computer Graphic Artist: Randy Kady
Production Manager: Gingar Kunkel

Library of Congress Cataloging-in-Publication Data

Training youth for dynamic leadership.
        p.   cm.
    Includes index.
    ISBN 0-7644-2074-7 (alk. paper)
    1. Christian leadership--Study and teaching. 2. Christian education of young people. I. Group Publishing.
BV652.1.T73 1998
259'.23--dc21   98-30159
                                                                                    CIP

10 9 8 7 6 5 4 3 2 1   08 07 06 05 04 03 02 01 00 99

Printed in the United States of America.

Contents

Introduction

How to Use This Resource

"When I look back on my life, I realize that God was preparing me every step of the way to be in Christian ministry," says Sandy. As an adult in Christian leadership, Sandy believes the leadership opportunities she had as a teenager gave her the preparation and motivation she needed to enter Christian ministry as an adult.

Sandy was raised in a churchgoing family in a small Midwestern town. Her church was small, too. In fact, Sandy's youth group consisted of six teenagers, only three of whom were active participants. And from the beginning, Sandy felt like an important member of that church.

Sandy's pastor recognized gifts and talents in Sandy and helped her develop those gifts in ministry. From the time she was in eighth grade, Sandy was the church organist. She often joined the pastor and others on visits to the hospital. She created posters and collages to publicize church events. She even attended area denominational events as a delegate for her church.

When Sandy was in high school, she served as a youth representative on an area committee for youth ministry. From there, she served as a representative for the state committee. Later on, she was chosen as the one teenage delegate to represent her state at the denomination's national event for adults and young people.

When Sandy was in college, she continued to increase her leadership responsibilities. For two years, she acted as a volunteer consultant to churches. On behalf of the regional office of her denomination, she traveled around to various churches to help them plan, assess, and train for their youth ministry programs. In the process, she worked with hundreds of youth leaders and thousands of teenagers. She also worked to plan districtwide youth events. As an adult, she ministers directly and indirectly to hundreds of thousands of people all over the world.

Sandy's life is an example of how leadership opportunities for young people can produce skilled adult leaders. Because she was granted increasing small leadership opportunities and encouraged to participate in them, Sandy gained the training she needed to enter full-time Christian ministry.

Because Sandy was given the opportunity to show faithfulness in the "small things," she is serving God faithfully today. All because one pastor took the time to invest in her.

In *Reaching a Generation for Christ,* Mark H. Senter III says, "Student ownership of youth ministry guided by respected Christian adults is essential for the ministry to remain healthy. Youth ministry begins when an adult earns the right to be heard by students, but it reaches its peak of effectiveness when the adult has earned the right to be silent. Students, willing and capable of providing spiritually sensitive leadership for the youth group, assume ownership. Seldom will a youth ministry reach the point where the students will have so much ownership and maturity that their adult leader will be able to remain entirely silent, but that should be the goal for at least some aspect of the ministry."

It's for this reason that we've created this book. *Training Youth for Dynamic Leadership* is a tool that will help you equip your young people for ownership of their youth ministry program. In fact, it's a tool kit. Check out what this book has to offer; then pull out the tools your students need to carry out their leadership responsibilities. Whether you want to teach your students to lead meetings, facilitate small-group discussions, counsel hurting peers, reach out to others, or lead by example, this book provides what you need to introduce basic principles of Christian leadership and to train your students to lead.

Putting Together a Training Program

This resource consists of several elements you can combine to customize a training program for your young people. It includes these mix-and-match elements:
- **Bible Studies—to give biblical background for leadership.**
- **Skill Sessions—to teach specific leadership skills.**
- **Retreat Plan—to help kids discover more about their own leadership gifts and styles.**
- **Checkup Sessions—to give kids an opportunity to support each other and to process issues that have come up in leadership.**
- **Basic Training Activities—to give kids a basic understanding of important aspects of leadership.** (The thirteen basic training activities are designed to be short and can be used throughout your leadership training program in partnership with other activities—at the end of a Bible study or a skill session, for example. Or you may want to use them individually in short meetings.)

You can use all the material provided, or you can pick and choose to concentrate on the skills your students need. For example, if you want to teach your young people how to lead small groups, you may want to start with a Bible study on servant leadership, followed by the basic training activity on communication skills (during the same session). Then you would move to the skill session on leading a small group, followed by the basic training activity on group dynamics. Next, you might follow the weekend retreat plan—with a concentration on small-group leadership skills. During your retreat, you would want to include the basic training activities on conflict resolution, listening, and affirmation. After the retreat, the five checkup sessions would provide ongoing support and training for students as they lead their small groups.

Use the elements in this book to create a program that works for you and your group. Be sure to take into consideration the purpose of your leadership training, the time period you want the training course to cover, and the particular needs of your student leaders. And remember, you can use the entire resource to provide great, well-rounded training on what Christian leadership is all about! (See the "Suggested Leadership Training Tracks" box on the following page for some specific suggestions.)

Suggested Leadership Training Tracks

Training Focus:
Leading Small-Group Meetings

Elements to Include:

Bible Study
- Servant Leadership (p. 8)

Skill Session
- Leading a Small Group (p. 27)

Retreat (p. 43)

Basic Training Activities
- Communication Skills (p. 80)
- Group Dynamics (p. 94)
- Conflict Resolution (p. 100)
- Listening (p. 103)
- Affirmation (p. 120)

Checkup Sessions (pp. 65-78)

Training Focus:
Reaching Out to Others

Elements to Include:

Bible Studies
- Servant Leadership (p. 8)
- Fruit of the Spirit (p. 15)

Skill Sessions
- Outreach (p. 33)
- Peer Counseling (p. 38)

Retreat (p. 43)

Basic Training Activities
- Communication Skills (p. 80)
- Role Modeling (p. 83)
- Listening (p. 103)
- Prayer (p. 116)
- Affirmation (p. 120)
- Integrity (p. 123)

Checkup Sessions (pp. 65-78)

Training Focus:
Leading Large-Group Meetings

Elements to Include:

Bible Studies
- Servant Leadership (p. 8)
- Fruit of the Spirit (p. 15)
- Spiritual Gifts (p. 19)

Skill Session
- Leading a Meeting (p. 23)

Retreat (p. 43)

Basic Training Activities
- Communication Skills (p. 80)
- Decision Making (p. 87)
- Delegating (p. 91)
- Group Dynamics (p. 94)
- Growing From Failure (p. 97)
- Listening (p. 103)
- Accountability (p. 106)
- Responsibility (p. 111)

Checkup Sessions (pp. 65-78)

Training Focus:
Leading by Example

Elements to Include:

Bible Studies
- Servant Leadership (p. 8)
- Fruit of the Spirit (p. 15)
- Spiritual Gifts (p. 19)

Skill Sessions
- Outreach (p. 33)
- Peer Counseling (p. 38)

Retreat (p. 43)

Basic Training Activities
- Communication Skills (p. 80)
- Role Modeling (p. 83)
- Conflict Resolution (p. 100)
- Listening (p. 103)
- Prayer (p. 116)
- Affirmation (p. 120)
- Integrity (p. 123)

Checkup Sessions (pp. 65-78)

Making the Most of the Handouts

The handouts provided in this book give some excellent overviews of leadership skills and personal characteristics your students will find valuable in leadership. Because most learning happens through experience, your students will retain the material better when they are actually in positions of leadership. For example, a student who learns an overview of what it means to resolve conflict may remember basic principles of that lesson, but when he or she is forced to handle a conflict in real life, those principles will become much more meaningful. The handouts in this book can provide tools to help students apply what they learn to real-life situations.

You may want to give each student a notebook to use to keep track of the handouts and notes from this training course. Or you may want to have students supply their own. Either way, it's a good idea to remind students to compile and keep the information they receive in this training course. You may even want to encourage students to decorate the covers of their notebooks to make them unique. The handouts will become excellent reference resources as they become Christian leaders.

One Last Note

Be careful of assuming that only those young people who already lead are leaders—these active leaders have simply already had opportunity to learn leadership. This book is designed to provide leadership skills and opportunities to kids with all kinds of spiritual gifts. Instead of picking specific young people to be leaders, recognize the leadership potential in every teenager. Invite each student to be a part of your leadership training program, conscious that God gifts every believer and that with God's guidance those gifts can grow.

Because leaders are grown, not born, we suggest that you commit to equip every student to lead if he or she wants to. Some will be more verbal leaders; others will be quieter. Some will be upfront leaders; others will lead within the group. But each is critical to your group and to God's kingdom. Each can take his or her designed-by-God place in your group and in the body of Christ.

May God bless you as you encourage your young people to take ownership of their group and to see themselves as essential members of the body of Christ.

Bible Studies

Use these Bible studies to give student leaders
biblical background for leadership.

Bible Study

Topic: Servant leadership

Scripture: Mark 10:35-45

Supplies: You'll need Bibles, newsprint, markers, masking tape, four copies of the "Who Is a Real Leader?" handout (p. 13), pens or pencils, paper, a whip or a big stick, and a chair or wooden box. You'll also need one nine-inch piece of thin satin (or leather) cord for each person and enough alphabet beads so each person can spell out the Greek word "doulos." You can find alphabet beads (beads with letters of the alphabet on them) at most craft stores.

Preparation: Before the session, study Mark 10:35-45. Then read the entire session outline. Make sure all the activities fit your group, and make any necessary changes. Make four photocopies of the "Who Is a Real Leader?" handout (p. 13). "Mess up" your meeting area before students arrive by scattering papers and hymnals on the floor, turning over chairs, and generally putting things where they don't belong. Finally, before the Bible study, select two students to serve as team leaders during the cleanup. Instruct one leader to order team members in an authoritarian way to clean and straighten their area. He or she can give everyone some task to do, such as putting paper in the trash can, arranging the chairs, or putting away hymnals, and can walk around watching the team and criticize the speed or quality of its work. Instruct the other leader to ask team members for their help as he or she begins to clean their area. Encourage the second leader to focus on serving rather than "leading," even helping the other team clean its area.

Overview:

This session offers a description of what it means to be a servant leader like Christ. Students will
- experience and discuss the pros and cons of different types of leadership;
- discover from Jesus' teaching the traits of servant (Christlike) leadership;
- apply the servant leadership model to real-life situations; and
- commit to being servant leaders in their youth group, church, schools, and homes.

Getting Started

When students arrive, tell them it will be difficult to conduct the session with the meeting area in such a mess, so you'd like them to form two work teams to clean up the area. Form two teams, asking each of the leaders you selected beforehand to assume responsibility for one team. Then assign each team one-half of the meeting area to clean.

After the meeting area has been cleaned, tell kids it's time to begin the session. Have kids form groups of four that contain two members from each team. Then say: **It's crucial for student leaders like you to understand what it means to be Christlike leaders. All too often, however, even Christian leaders treat people as I asked** (name of first team leader) **to treat the members of his** (or her) **team. So we're going to devote this session to discovering how to become servant leaders just like Jesus.**

Have group members discuss the following questions. After each question, ask volunteers to report their groups' responses. Ask:

● **What emotions were you feeling as you were cleaning up your area?**

● **How did your team leader's attitude affect the way you tended to work?**

● **When have you been bossed around by an authoritarian leader?**

● **How do authoritarian leaders affect the people they're leading? the work those people do?**

Understanding God's Word

Say: **No one likes to be ordered around by leaders. Unfortunately, sometimes even Christians seem to think that being an effective leader means telling people what to do and how to do it. But that isn't the kind of leader Jesus was, and it shouldn't be the kind of leaders we are. Let's read what Jesus said in Mark 10 about being a leader.**

Make sure each group has a Bible. Then ask group members to read Mark 10:35-45 together. Allow several minutes for reading; then ask the following questions. After each question, ask volunteers to report their groups' answers. Ask:

● **Why do you think James and John asked what they did?**

● **What are some reasons you want to be a leader?**

● **Why do you think the other disciples became indignant?**

● **How have others reacted to your attempts at leadership?**

● **According to Jesus, what makes someone a truly great leader?**

● **How do you think Jesus would have led your work team?**

Then give each group two sheets of newsprint and a marker. Have groups draw the outline of a person on each sheet of newsprint and label one "authoritarian leader" and the other "servant leader." Tell groups they have five minutes to write on their pieces of newsprint how an authoritarian leader and a servant leader are different. For example, kids might write "looks for ways to serve" by the servant leader's eyes and "watches just to criticize" by the authoritarian leader's eyes, or "beats people down" by the authoritarian leader's hands and "lifts people up" by the servant leader's hands.

After five minutes, ask small groups to hang their pieces of newsprint and share their descriptions. Then say: **It's easy for us to say that we are to be servant** leaders like Jesus or to describe what a servant leader would look like. It's not so easy, however, to actually serve others when we find ourselves in a leadership position. So let's take some time to discuss how we can be servant leaders in various situations of life.

Applying the Bible

Have students form four groups based on where they would most like to be servant leaders: in the youth group, at church, at school, or in the home. If groups are unequal in size, ask members of some groups to move to their second choices to create fairly equal-sized groups.

Give each group a copy of the "Who Is a Real Leader?" handout, a pen or pencil, and a sheet of paper. Assign situation one to the students in the youth group, situation two to the church group, situation three to the school group, and situation four to the home group. Instruct group members to read the situation (which tells how an authoritarian leader would handle a particular task), to list what is specifically wrong with that person's leadership, and to describe how Jesus—our model servant leader—would handle the situation.

Allow groups to work for five to ten minutes; then ask groups to take turns reading their situations and reporting their results. Then ask the entire group the following questions:

● **When have you been in situations like the ones just described?**

● **When have you been an authoritarian leader like the one on the newsprint? a servant leader?**

● **What makes it difficult for you to be a servant? to be a leader?**

● **What will help you remember to be a servant leader like Jesus?**

Closing

Say: **Sometimes the way we view or symbolize leadership tends to influence the way we act as a leader. For example, if we think of leadership as** (hold up a whip or a big stick) **"whipping (or 'beating') followers into shape,"** **we focus so much on our goal that we fail to serve those placed in our care.** **Or if we think leaders are on a pedestal** (stand on a chair or a wooden box), **we forget that Jesus tells us to lower ourselves to those below us.**

Ask the entire group:

● **What are some symbols that would remind us to be servants?**

Allow kids to share their ideas, and then say: **In Jesus' day, servants and slaves were sometimes shackled to control where they went and what they did. The bonds reminded servants of their responsibility to serve others. In a similar way, we can create our own symbols of servant leadership to remind us that we are servants of Jesus and of everyone he puts under our care.**

Set out the satin cord and the alphabet beads. Instruct each person to take one length of cord and the letters to spell out "doulos." Have kids slide the beads onto the cords to spell out the word "doulos" and then knot the cords so they fit their wrists. While kids are working, explain that "doulos" is the Greek word for "servant" or "slave" and that the Bible instructs us to become Christlike leaders by being servants to others (Mark 10:43-45).

When kids finish, say: **Every time you see your "doulos bracelet," you'll be reminded to lead as Jesus would lead, by serving those who look to you for leadership.** Then encourage young people to wear the doulos bracelets as a commitment to lead as Jesus would—through service. Encourage kids to spend a moment in a silent prayer of commitment. Then conclude the session in prayer, thanking God for the leadership example of Jesus and dedicating the members of the group to his service.

Handout: Who is a Real Leader?

Read the situation that corresponds to your group. Then list what is wrong with the authoritarian leadership depicted, and explain how Jesus would exercise leadership in that situation.

1. Leading the Troops in Retreat

It's time for the annual ski retreat, and Mary knows exactly what needs to be done. She's assigned each group member to a committee and given each committee leader (whom she appointed on the basis of his or her "spirituality") a list of the supplies and tasks the committee is responsible for. Everyone knows what to do and when to do it. Mary has taken responsibility for selecting a retreat site, arranging for a retreat speaker, and collecting the food and lodging fees from people attending. Everything is ready, and this retreat promises to be, like those in years past, a model of machinelike efficiency.

2. Taking the Lead at Church

Mike, the church youth leader, passionately believes he needs to get everyone in the group involved in ministry. Because Mike has a special burden for feeding homeless people, he challenges "his kids" every week to contribute a portion of their paychecks or allowances to a special homeless food fund. Also, one week every month, Mike cancels the regular youth meeting and tells kids to meet him at the local food bank to serve meals to homeless people. If group members don't show up, Mike calls them and reminds them of their obligation to feed the hungry (Matthew 25:34-40).

3. Leading the Way to a Good Grade

Ms. Buchanan, the high school history teacher, has just assigned class members to groups that will prepare and present reports on the Vietnam War. Linda has aced every quiz and exam in the course, so the members of her group choose her to lead them. Fearful that her grade might suffer from the inadequacies of her group members, Linda decides to take matters into her own hands. She writes seven questions the report will answer, assigns one question to each group member (retaining four for herself), and tells each person where to research his or her question. Linda also states that she will create overhead transparencies to present their insights. For the sake of simplicity, Linda will present the group's findings, mentioning each person's part in creating the report.

4. "Head" of the House

John, the oldest of four children, has been asked to take care of his two sisters and brother while their parents spend the weekend at a marriage seminar. John wants to prove to his parents that he can be trusted, so he wrote out a list of "house rules" about where his siblings can go, when they are to be back, when they must work on homework, and how much TV they can watch. John also assigned everyone else specific jobs, such as cleaning the bathroom, dusting the living room, and raking the lawn. John is determined that when his parents return, they'll see that the house is in better order than when they left.

Bible Study

Topic: Fruit of the Spirit

Scripture: John 15:1-11; Galatians 5:16-23

Supplies: You'll need one lemon, one grapefruit, and one orange for every twenty people in your group. For every group of five, you'll also need a blindfold, a sheet of newsprint, and markers. For every person you'll need a Bible, a photocopy of the "Fruit of the Spirit" handout (p. 18), a pen or pencil, and paper.

Preparation: Study Galatians 5 and John 15. Read through the session, making sure all the activities will work with your group, and make any necessary changes. Make one photocopy of the "Fruit of the Spirit" handout (p. 18) for each person in the group.

Overview:

This session provides an introduction to the importance of cultivating the fruit of the Spirit in leadership. Students will
- discover what the fruit of the Spirit is,
- learn how to cultivate these characteristics in their lives,
- see the important role these play in leadership, and
- check the status of fruit in their own lives.

Getting Started

Have students form groups of five, and give each group a blindfold. Have each group blindfold the oldest person in the group. Then give each group a slice of lemon, a slice of grapefruit, and a slice of orange. Tell the blindfolded people that they're the fruit testers and they'll have three opportunities to demonstrate their prowess.

Have the fruit testers plug their noses while other members of their groups feed them the slices of grapefruit. Have each fruit tester guess what the fruit is. Then have the fruit testers taste the slice of lemon without plugging their noses (but still blindfolded). Have them guess what that fruit is. Then give them a chance to taste and identify the slice of orange without the blindfolds.

When all the groups have finished, ask:
- **What was the easiest fruit to identify? Why?**
- **Why were some fruits more difficult to identify?**
- **In what ways does this activity relate to identifying the fruit of the Spirit in our own lives? In other people's lives?**

Understanding God's Word

Say: **Sometimes the work of the Holy Spirit is so evident in a person's life that it is very easy to see or identify. In other cases, it takes a close inspection of the person's character to see it. Let's take a look at two passages of Scripture that tell us what the fruit of the Spirit is and how we can cultivate a "fruit-filled" life. First let's read Galatians 5:16-23.**

In their original groups of five, have students read Galatians 5:16-23. Then ask the following questions, giving groups time to discuss each question after you ask it:

● **From this passage, what is the key to having a fruit-filled life?**

● **Have you ever known any spiritual leaders who demonstrated more deeds of the flesh than fruit of the Spirit? What did you think of that?**

● **Why is the fruit of the Spirit so important for leadership?**

● **How can we cultivate the fruit in our lives?**

Next have groups read John 15:1-11, and discuss the following questions:

● **According to this passage, what is the key to bearing fruit?**

● **What does God do when we bear fruit? What does it feel like? What are the benefits for leaders?**

● **What did Jesus mean when he said, "remain in me" and "remain in my love"? How do we do that?**

Applying the Bible

Say: **Just as fruit has to have the proper conditions to grow, so does the fruit of the Spirit. Take a look at this handout, look up the Scripture passages, and write down ways you can cultivate each fruit in your leadership.**

Have students form new groups of five. Give each person a photocopy of the "Fruit of the Spirit" handout and a pen or pencil. Assign each group three of the fruits to focus on (it's OK to duplicate).

When everyone is finished, have groups share what they learned and talk about the ideas they came up with. Encourage students to complete their handouts with the ideas the other groups share.

Closing

Give each group a sheet of newsprint and several markers. Have each member of the group choose one of the spiritual fruits that he or she will cultivate in leadership in the near future. Have each person draw the corresponding fruit from the list below and then write the name of a person he or she plans to demonstrate that fruit toward at the next meeting. Use the following list of fruits:

Love—Lemon

Joy—"Juicy Fruit" (watermelon)

Peace—Peach
Patience—Plum
Kindness—Kiwi
Goodness—Guava
Faithfulness—Fig
Gentleness—Grape
Self-Control—Strawberry

"**But** the fruit of the Spirit is love, joy, peace, patience, kindness, goodness, faithfulness, gentleness and self-control. Against such things there is no law."

Galatians 5:22-23

Handout
Fruit of the Spirit

Fruit	Scripture Reference	How I Can Cultivate
Love	Matthew 22:37-39	
Joy	Philippians 4:4	
Peace	1 Peter 3:11	
Patience	1 Thessalonians 5:14	
Kindness	Colossians 3:12	
Goodness	Galatians 6:10	
Faithfulness	Revelation 2:10	
Gentleness	Colossians 3:12	
Self-Control	2 Peter 1:5-6	

Bible Study

Topic: Spiritual gifts

Scripture: Romans 12:3-8 and 1 Corinthians 12:4-11

Supplies: You'll need one inexpensive gift for each person, wrapping paper, transparent tape, scissors, Bibles, newsprint, masking tape, markers, paper, pens or pencils, Bible encyclopedias, resource books on the spiritual gifts (such as *How to Discover Your Spiritual Gifts* by Clyde B. McDowell or *Spiritual Gifts* by Charles R. Swindoll), index cards, construction paper, and glue.

Preparation: Before the session, study Romans 12:3-8; 1 Corinthians 12:4-11; and resources on the spiritual gifts. Then read the entire session outline. Make sure all the activities fit your group, and make any necessary changes. Finally, wrap one gift for each person. Gifts might include loose change, a picture of a smile, a blank thank-you card, a heart plaque, or even toilet paper. Participants will use the gifts to serve each other during the session. Set the gifts out where students will see them.

Overview:

This session introduces young people to the spiritual gifts and to their proper use. Students will:
- receive special gifts and then use those gifts to serve others in the group,
- discover what the spiritual gifts are and how God wants them to use them,
- identify their spiritual gifts and ways those gifts can be used in the group, and
- commit to using their spiritual gifts to serve and lead others in the youth group.

Getting Started

When everyone has arrived, ask kids to form groups of four and to discuss the following questions:
- **What was the best gift you've ever received?**
- **What did you do with the gift after you got it?**
- **What's the best gift you've ever given someone?**
- **What did the recipient do with the gift you gave?**

Say: **Everyone likes to receive nice gifts. And when we receive the perfect present, we know that the person who gave it cares about us enough to have looked for just the right gift to show that love to us. Because I care for each of you very much, I'd like to give each one of you a special gift. My only request is that you don't let anyone else know what gift you receive.**

Distribute the gifts and allow kids several minutes to open and secretly look at their gifts. Then instruct students to close up their gifts and to discuss the following questions within their groups:

- **What do you think of the gift you received?**
- **Would you share your gift with others? Why or why not?**

Understanding God's Word

Say: **When we receive a wonderful gift, we often feel so good that we want to share our excitement (and even our gift) with others. And that's exactly what God wants us to do with the gifts he gives us. Let's learn about some of the gifts God has already given us.**

Have group members read Romans 12:3-8 and 1 Corinthians 12:4-11 and then discuss the following questions:

- **In light of these passages, how would you define "spiritual gift"?**
- **What do these passages say about who has received spiritual gifts?**
- **What should be our attitude toward the gifts that God has given us?**
- **According to these verses, what is the purpose of the spiritual gifts?**

Say: **God gave each of us one or more spiritual gifts, not so we could hold those gifts close and keep them for ourselves, but so we would share them with others for their good. Of course, this raises several questions: What are those gifts, and which ones has God given to us personally?**

Have kids stay in their groups. Then hang several sheets of newsprint and have kids call out the gifts listed in Romans 12:3-8 and 1 Corinthians 12:4-11. Write those gifts on the newsprint, leaving space to write under each gift.

When all the gifts have been called out, give each group several sheets of paper and a pen or pencil. Then assign each group (or allow each group to choose) several of the spiritual gifts, making sure all the gifts are assigned. Set out the Bible encyclopedias and resources on the spiritual gifts. Tell groups they have five minutes to find and write out definitions of their assigned gifts.

After five minutes, have groups take turns reporting what they learned. Write the definitions on the newsprint. Allow groups to ask for clarification about any definitions they don't fully understand.

When all the gifts have been defined, ask the entire group:

- **Do you think God gives other spiritual gifts not listed in these passages? If so, what might they be?** Write kids' ideas on the newsprint.

Applying the Bible

Say: **God gave each one of you at least one spiritual gift to share with others, to use as a means of serving others. So let's spend some time trying to discover what spiritual gifts God has given us.**

Have kids spend several minutes in quiet reflection, thinking about the following questions. Pause for about thirty seconds to one minute after each question. Ask:

- **What special talents or abilities has God given you?**
- **How have you used those abilities to minister to others?**
- **What special concerns or burdens do you feel for others?**
- **How could you use your abilities to address those concerns?**
- **What spiritual gifts might your abilities and concerns point to?**

Give each person an index card and a pen or pencil. Ask kids to write the answers to the last question on their index cards. Then invite group members to share with each other what they discovered and wrote. Encourage students to suggest other spiritual gifts they see in each other.

After five to ten minutes, say: **At times we may feel that some gifts are better than others, but that's not God's perspective.** Read aloud 1 Corinthians 12:14-25. Then say: **Some of you may feel that the gift I gave you earlier is silly or unimportant, but each one of those gifts can be shared with others. Each gift can be used to do something positive for others.**

Set out the markers, tape, scissors, construction paper, and glue. Tell kids that they have five minutes to use the gifts you gave them to serve or do something positive for each other. Encourage kids to make sure everyone is the recipient of a "gift." If kids seem to have difficulty thinking of ways to use their gifts, suggest possibilities such as creating an encouraging card, making a meaningful object, or using the gift to perform a kind deed.

After five minutes, ask volunteers to report ways they were served or encouraged by others' gifts. Then ask the entire group the following questions:

- **How were you encouraged by receiving others' gifts?**
- **How did you benefit by giving your gift to others?**

Closing

Say: **Just as you used the gift I gave you earlier to serve others, you can use the spiritual gifts God has given you to help and serve others.**

Ask kids to suggest ways to use each spiritual gift listed on the newsprint in a student leadership position. Write kids' ideas on the newsprint. Then ask kids to walk to the newsprint and write their names next to the spiritual gifts they believe they have.

When everyone has written his or her name by at least one gift, ask kids to write on their index cards ways they will use their spiritual gifts to serve the members of the entire youth group.

When kids finish writing their commitments, have them tape the index cards to gifts they received, either from you or from other people. Then ask kids to re-form their original groups and to close in a prayer of thanks to God for their spiritual gifts and of commitment to use those gifts to serve others in the youth group.

Encourage kids to put their gifts where they'll see them often as reminders of God's gifts to them and of their duty to use those gifts to serve others.

Skill Sessions

Use these skill sessions to teach student leaders
to use their leadership skills in specific ways.

Skill Session

Topic: Leading a meeting

Supplies: You'll need modeling clay, blindfolds, photocopies of the "Meeting Planner" handout (p. 26), Bibles, pens or pencils, newsprint, tape, paper, and markers.

Preparation: Make a simple shape out of modeling clay. Hide the shape until the "assemblers" are blindfolded. Make three photocopies of the "Meeting Planner" handout (p. 26) for each person.

Opener

Have kids form pairs. One partner should be the assembler, and the other should be the foreman. Give each pair a blindfold, and have the foremen blindfold their assemblers. Once assemblers are blindfolded, show the foremen the modeling-clay creation you made earlier. Give some modeling clay to each assembler, and ask foremen to describe the creation to their assemblers. Ask the assemblers to create the shape their foremen are describing. Give pairs three minutes to attempt this.

When time is up, have assemblers remove their blindfolds and see how close their creations came to the real thing. Ask:

● **When have you tried something and felt like you faced a barrier to accomplishing it?**

● **When have you tried to explain an idea and felt like your audience wasn't understanding you?**

Say: **Sometimes teaching the Bible can feel like this exercise. We might make a good attempt at teaching a great spiritual truth and fail because we lack understanding of some basic principles. For example, if we change just a few basic elements in our game, creating a shape like the one I created in advance becomes easy.**

Repeat the exercise, but this time allow the assemblers to look closely at the shape you created. Then, with their eyes shut, they can attempt to create the shape again. Say: **When we're allowed to see how an object has been created, making something like it can become easier. One important skill for many effective leaders is the ability to lead effective meetings. Today we're going to zero in on how to plan a meeting, and we'll talk about some strategies that will make us better teachers too.**

Understanding the Skills

Say: **I'd like to focus on two essentials in meeting development. We'll talk**

about a basic teaching strategy; then we'll discuss how to plan and structure a meeting.

Have students form four groups. Place a Bible and some pens or pencils in each of four locations in your meeting room. Ask each group to go sit in a circle around one of the Bibles. Ask groups to read 2 Kings 2:1-12 aloud in their groups. Say: **When we teach, our goal should be to present ideas, experiences, and information in a way that helps our learners understand them and apply them to their lives. An essential element in leading a meeting is teaching so your learners will really learn.**

Humans are interesting creations. We each learn primarily in one of four ways. We usually learn by hearing, seeing, doing, or reading. I'm going to assign each group one of these learning modes. I'd like you to present the truth in 2 Kings 2:1-12 in the way that I assign you. When you're finished, we'll talk about your teaching method.

Assign each group one of these learning modes: hearing, seeing, doing, or reading. Give each person a photocopy of the "Meeting Planner" handout. Encourage kids to refer to the "Four Elements Effective Teachers Use" section of their handouts for ideas. While students are preparing their presentations, make yourself available for questions.

When groups are finished preparing, have each group make its presentation. After each presentation, ask the audience:

● **What did you learn?**

● **How interested were you as the passage was being presented?**

When all groups are finished presenting, say: **It's absolutely important that you include every one of these learning styles in your teaching strategy, since you'll probably have learners of all types in every group you lead.**

Say: **With your group, make a plan to reteach the passage using all four of these learning strategies. I'm not going to ask you to teach again, but I'd like you to make a plan to present to the entire group.**

When groups are finished, gather everyone together. Ask groups to present their strategies to everyone else.

Say: **Congratulations! You've learned the importance of including different types of learners. Now let's look at the second part of developing a meeting: meeting essentials.**

Have kids form groups of four. Direct students to the "Bare-Bones Meeting Essentials" segment of their handouts. Say: **Planning a meeting is a tough but important process. In a moment, you'll have a chance to work through this process in your groups. Before you begin, I'd like you to read through the list of meeting essentials on your handout in order to get a handle on what you're going to do.**

While students are reading, give each group a sheet of newsprint, a marker, and a topic idea such as sharing your faith, reasons to believe in God, honoring your parents, or loving your neighbor. Ask groups to use the "Developing a Meeting" chart on their handouts as a guide as they plan their meetings. Instruct groups to be creative and add elements that they feel are great ideas. Also, instruct students to add people who might be good at leading various aspects of the meeting.

When groups are finished, have each group present its idea and chart and then tape the chart to a wall in your meeting room. When the presentations are finished, Say: **Now, let's spend some time comparing. What do you like about what you've seen?**

Encourage students to engage in an open discussion of the elements they like from each of the meeting ideas. Give a volunteer paper and a pen so he or she can act as recorder, making notes of what elements people highlight.

Closing

Say: **Let's talk about one other essential before we go. I'd like you to do some quick brainstorming of topics you think are essential for teenagers to study. As you shout them out, I'll write them on newsprint. I encourage you to write them on the back of your handout so you'll remember some topic ideas.**

Give students time to brainstorm about topic ideas. When they're finished say: **I'd like to hear your reactions to what you've heard today. I'm going to give you a few minutes to shout out one or two new things that you have learned today.**

Allow students time to mention their new ideas. When they're finished, say: **I'm very proud of you! You've learned how to lead a meeting, and you've grasped some of the basic elements of how to teach others so that they'll learn and understand what God's Word says. I can't wait to see how you use this information and how God uses you as you lead meetings.**

Close your meeting with a time of prayer, asking God to give your leaders strength and creativity as they lead others in the discovery of God's Word. Give each student two more copies of the "Meeting Planner" handout to use in planning future meetings.

Four Elements Effective Teachers Use

1. Doing—Some people learn most effectively by physically participating in activities. **Ideas:** acting, drawing, games, crafts.

2. Reading—Some people learn effectively by reading whatever they're trying to learn. **Ideas:** Small-group reading, individual reading, dramatic reading, creating (and then reading aloud) stories, overhead transparencies.

3. Seeing—Many people grasp truth by seeing it acted out or demonstrated. These people learn visually. **Ideas:** Dramas, videos, advertising, real-life situations, artwork, watching interviews, diagrams, posters.

4. Hearing— An auditory learner grasps ideas by listening to them being read or discussed. Many times these people also learn by reading aloud to themselves or others. **Ideas:** Reading stories, singing, listening to music, hearing sermons.

Bare-Bones Meeting Essentials

- a way to introduce the topic
- group interaction
- instruction from God's Word
- a spiritual element, including prayer
- smooth transitions between elements of the meeting
- a conclusion

Nonessential Meeting Extras

- games/crowdbreakers
- singing
- snacks
- videos
- skits
- music
- affirmation and encouragement

Developing a Meeting

Meeting Element	What	When	Who
Introduction			
Group interaction			
God's Word			
Conclusion			
Prayer			
Extra element			
Extra element			
Extra element			
Extra element			

Skill Session

Topic: Leading a small group

Supplies: You'll need photocopies of the "Leading a Small Group" handout (p. 31), photocopies of the "Putting a Meeting Together" handout (p. 32), newsprint, a marker, and tape.

Preparation: Make one photocopy of the "Leading a Small Group" handout (p. 31) for each student and a photocopy of the "Putting a Meeting Together" (p. 32) handout for each student. List these characteristics of small groups on a sheet of newsprint: build relationships, help people grow in Christ, encourage people to express themselves, give people living examples of what it means to be a Christian.

Opener

Say: **I'd like you to listen to the following comment, and then tell me what you think of it: "Me, join a small group? I don't think so. Gimme a huge youth activity, a crowded stadium, or a packed-out Christian concert. That's where it's at. Small groups are too confining."**

Ask:

● **What's your reaction to this comment?**
● **Why do some people avoid small groups?**
● **Why are small groups important?**

When students have shared several answers, say: **You've come up with some great reasons why small groups are important. I think the importance of small groups can be summed up in four basic characteristics of small groups: They build relationships, they help people grow in Christ, they encourage people to express themselves, and they give people living examples of what it means to be a Christian.**

Tape to the wall the piece of newsprint you wrote the four characteristics on before this session. Say: **The four characteristics that make small groups important also define the mission of a small-group leader. A leader's mission is to build relationships, to help people grow in Christ, to encourage people to express themselves, and to give people a living example of what it means to be a Christian.**

Have students form groups of two or three, and assign each group one aspect of the fourfold mission you just described. It's OK to assign each aspect to more than one group. Encourage groups to spend some time thinking of reasons their assigned aspects of the mission are important. After a few minutes, allow each group to express its thoughts to everyone else.

When each group has had an opportunity to share, say: **Now let's take a look at the specific responsibilities of a small-group leader.**

Understanding the Skills

Say: **Before a small-group meeting begins, it's important to understand the importance of vision and preparation. A good leader catches a vision for the group and prepares for it long before a meeting begins.**

Like a compass, a vision keeps your group on course. It's important to have in mind the purpose and goals of the group. Let's take some time to think through that now. Have students stay in their small groups from the previous activity, and encourage each student to answer the following questions.

- **What do you visualize your group doing or becoming on a regular basis?**
- **What is your desired outcome after the first meeting?**
- **How will the group evolve in one month? In six months?**
- **What do you see as the long-term results?**

After a few minutes, bring everyone together, and allow volunteers to share their answers.

Say: **Once you've thought through the vision for your group, the next step is to prepare for the meeting. Let's practice preparing for the small groups you'll be leading.** Again, have each person answer these questions in a small group:

- **Where will your small group meet?**
- **What potential distractions are at this location?**
- **As the leader, where will you sit to minimize those distractions?**
- **What can you do to make everyone in your group most comfortable?**
- **How will people know where to meet?**
- **Where will people park their cars?**
- **What will the timetable for your meeting look like?**
- **What methods of ministry will you use in your group?**

Bring everyone together again to share answers, and then ask:

- **How can small-group leaders prepare themselves spiritually for meetings?**
- **How might that spiritual preparation affect a small-group meeting?**
- **How can a leader create a friendly, nonthreatening environment?**

Say: **Once the meeting begins, a good leader helps the meeting flow smoothly. I'm going to give you some practical suggestions that will help keep people on course and moving together toward your group's goal.**

Say: **Start the meeting powerfully and on time.** Write this tip on a piece of newsprint and tape it to the wall.

Say: **Weak beginnings make everyone feel insecure. And meetings that start late encourage late people to be even later. Waiting for more people to** arrive rewards those who are late and indirectly communicates that everyone present isn't quite important enough to begin the meeting.

Say: **Set the course.** Write this tip on your piece of newsprint, below the previous tip.

Say: **Let group members know what to expect. If you want discussion, let them know ahead of time. Whether it's personal stories, prayer, worship, or something else, let the group know what's expected of them.**

Say: **Get people talking.** Add this tip to your newsprint list.

Say: **There's nothing worse than a mute group. Make sure your topics are relevant and your methods inviting. Be creative. Avoid asking dull questions like "Well, does anyone want to share?" Instead ask, "If Jesus were here today, what would he say to us?" If you want people to share their problems, you might say, "Let's go around the circle and allow everyone to tell us the greatest challenge he or she is facing today." Be sure your questions are open-ended and invite responses.**

Say: **Lead a discussion.** Add this tip to your newsprint list.

Say: **The role of a discussion leader is to keep the discussion moving and on course. Encourage everyone to participate, and keep your own words to a minimum. Always keep your objective in mind, and attempt to bring closure at the end. A good discussion leaves people satisfied but still hungry for more.**

Say: **Encourage prayer requests.** Add this tip to your newsprint list.

Say: **Transparency is challenging, especially for people who are new or just visiting. Do your best to create an environment of trust where genuine concern prevails. Show others that you care, and don't be afraid to talk about your own struggles. Always allow the Holy Spirit time to touch people.**

When your list is complete, ask students to form groups of five. If necessary, have some groups of four or six. If you have fewer than eight people in your group, do this activity as one group. Have each person in the group select one of the tasks you just discussed. In groups of four, have one person take two tasks. In groups of six, have two people share one task.

Have each group participate in a mock small group. Each student in the group should practice the task he or she chose. In other words, have one student start the meeting, one give an overview for the meeting, one initiate sharing, one lead a discussion, and one student encourage prayer requests.

Give groups two minutes for each task, calling time after each one so groups know when to move on to the next person.

When groups are finished, say: **Often the way a meeting ends determines whether people will return next time. I'd like to share some practical suggestions to end well.**

Discuss the following principles. Just as before, write them down one at a time where everyone can see them.

Say: **Leave people hungry for more instead of too full.**

Try not to make too many good things happen all at once. You don't

need to tell the group everything you know in the first meeting. If people are tired of sitting, end it. There's nothing worse than a leader dragging something out when everyone else is peeking at their watches.

Say: **Bring closure.**

Avoid unanswered questions or unresolved tension. Tie up loose ends and summarize all major points. Don't let people leave hurt and frustrated due to a bewildering comment. If necessary, pull individuals aside and talk with them after the meeting. Always end in prayer, with the final focus on one's relationship with Jesus Christ.

Say: **Make time for ministry after the meeting.**

Often what goes on after a meeting is as important as the meeting itself. Someone may have been touched by something said and may wait for others to leave in order to talk with you. Make yourself available for prayer and fellowship. Good leaders are often the first to arrive and the last to leave.

When everyone understands the three principles, ask for three volunteers who don't mind doing some spontaneous acting. Have each one role play the negative opposite of one of the principles you just discussed. For example, have one play the leader who crams too much into one meeting, while another leaves the group frustrated and bewildered due to a lack of closure. Have the third one play the role of an insensitive leader who ends the meeting terribly.

When volunteers are finished, lead the rest of the group in a round of applause, and then ask:

● **Have you ever experienced an ending like the ones our volunteers portrayed? How did that experience affect you?**

● **Why do you think it's so important to end a meeting well?**

● **What can you do to prepare to minister to those who might stay after a meeting to talk with you?**

Closing

Give each person a photocopy of the "Leading a Small Group" handout and a photocopy of the "Putting a Meeting Together" handout. Explain that the "Leading a Small Group" handout summarizes all the major points you discussed in this Skill Session. The "Putting a Meeting Together" handout will help student leaders plan thoroughly for a meeting. Encourage students to take their handouts with them when they leave.

Have students form a circle and hold hands. Close the meeting in prayer, encouraging students to pray aloud if they wish to. Ask God to help student leaders prepare appropriately and rely on God when leading small groups.

After the meeting, as necessary, minister to student leaders' personal needs.

Leading a Small Group

The Mission of a Small-Group Leader

- Build relationships.
- Help people grow in Christ.
- Encourage people to express themselves.
- Give people a living example of what it means to be a Christian.

Before a Meeting Begins

- Know your vision so you can keep your group on course.
- Prepare your meeting location and minimize distractions.
- Choose the method of ministry and the timetable for your meeting.
- Pray and prepare yourself spiritually.

During the Meeting

- Start the meeting powerfully and on time.
- Set the course, letting group members know what to expect.
- Get people talking through relevant and creative discussion.
- Lead a discussion, keeping your comments to a minimum.
- Encourage honest prayer requests.

Ending the Meeting

- Leave people hungry for more instead of trying to cram in too much.
- Bring closure, addressing any questions and any unresolved tension.
- Make time for ministry after the meeting.

Putting a Meeting Together

1. Which of the four meeting characteristics will you emphasize most in your next meeting? (Number them 1 through 4, in order of priority.)

_____Build relationships.

_____Help people grow in Christ.

_____Encourage people to express themselves.

_____Give people a living example of what it means to be a Christian.

2. What do you visualize your group doing or becoming during the meeting?

3. What long-term benefits do you hope will come about in your group?

4. What topic or subject matter will you introduce in the next meeting?

5. What methods of ministry will you use? (Circle one or more.)

teaching	video
discussion	music
personal stories	guest speaker
worship	handout
prayer	informal fellowship
other:_____	

6. As a leader, what do you see as your greatest challenge?

7. What can you do ahead of time to minimize problems?

8. How would you like the meeting to end?

9. What do you anticipate happening after the meeting is over?

Skill Session

Topic: Outreach

Supplies: You'll need photocopies of the "Key Skills for Effective Outreach" handout (pp. 36-37), store-bought invitations or card-stock paper and markers, pens or pencils, index cards, Bibles, newsprint, a marker, tape, and a chair.

Preparation: Make one photocopy of the "Key Skills for Effective Outreach" handout (pp. 36-37) for each person. Make or buy invitation cards that say "You Are Invited" on the outside. They should be blank on the inside. You'll need one invitation per student.

Opener

Give each person a photocopy of the "Key Skills for Effective Outreach" handout. Encourage students to use this handout to take notes throughout the session.

Give each student an invitation card and a pen or pencil. Say: **I'd like each of you to pretend you're writing an invitation to a good friend. Think about how you would go about inviting this friend to an upcoming party.**

Allow teenagers three to five minutes to complete their invitations. When kids are finished, ask volunteers to read their invitations aloud to the group.

Say: **Outreach doesn't have to be difficult. In fact, it can be fun. Inviting someone to be a part of a youth group event or part of the body of Christ is like inviting a friend to a party where Jesus is the host.** Then ask:

● **When are some times you've received invitations to events?**

● **Why did you decide to accept or decline those invitations?**

● **What feelings or factors were associated with your decisions to attend or not to attend?**

● **What are some key words and phrases you used in your invitation to reach out to your friend?** (Encourage students to write these words in the space after question 1 on their "Key Skills for Effective Outreach" handouts.)

Understanding the Skills

Give each student an index card and a pen or pencil. Make sure each person has a Bible. Ask a volunteer to read Acts 2:42-47.

Say: **The early Christians practiced much hospitality and friendship in their outreach to others. Their outreach was simple, not complex. We can make our outreach simple too.**

Ask:

● **How did the early church practice outreach, according to this Scripture passage in Acts?**

● **What principles might we apply to our outreach today?** (Encourage students to write their answers to this question in the space after question 2 on their "Key Skills for Effective Outreach" handouts.

Have students form groups of three to five. Ask the groups to brainstorm and write down on their index cards some simple ways the youth group might use principles from Acts 2:42-47 to reach out to others.

After five to seven minutes, collect the index cards. Then read aloud the ideas kids wrote on the index cards. Discuss each idea, and make a list on newsprint of those outreach ideas that seem to be particularly appealing to the students. (Encourage students to write these outreach ideas in the space after question 3 on their "Key Skills for Effective Outreach" handouts.)

Then say: **Now let's practice using some of these outreach ideas and develop them into skills. Let's do some role-playing and discuss how to make our outreach more effective.**

Invite students to role play several of the ideas. For example, your students may have decided that making telephone calls to other teenagers would be effective outreach. Invite two students to role play a telephone conversation—one playing the caller, and the other the teenager he or she is trying to reach out to. Ask the other students to listen to the conversation and make helpful comments and suggestions. If time allows, have students role play several of these conversations and talk about effective words and phrases to use.

After role-playing and discussing several outreach scenarios, ask:

● **Why is it important to reach out to others?** (Encourage students to write their answers to this question in the space after question 4 on their "Key Skills for Effective Outreach" handouts.)

● **How can we show the love of Jesus when we reach out to others?**

● **What do you think should be our goals in reaching out to others?**

Make a list of these goals on newsprint, and post them where everyone can see them. (Encourage students to write these goals in the space after question 5 on their "Key Skills for Effective Outreach" handouts.)

● **What are some skills you learned from the role-playing exercise that you can begin to practice?** (Encourage students to write their answers to these questions in the space after question 6 on their "Key Skills for Effective Outreach" handouts.)

Closing

Have students form a circle. Place an empty chair inside the circle.

Say: **Every time we meet, someone is missing. There is always another person who could be a part of our group, who needs the love and hope we have.**

Ask:

● **Can you think of other teenagers who might need the support our group has to offer?**

● **Why do you think those people are missing from our group?**

Say: **Let's work together to formulate a list of those teenagers so we can try to use some of the skills we learned today to invite them to be a part of our group.**

Hang a piece of newsprint on the wall. As kids call out names, list them on the newsprint. Then have students form a semicircle around the list, join hands, and pray aloud for the people on the list. When students have prayed, read Psalm 146 aloud as a closing prayer.

Encourage kids to take their "Key Skills for Effective Outreach" handouts with them to use as reference guides when they begin to use the skills they learned in this session.

Handout
Key Skills for Effective
Outreach

1. **Be real.** Outreach isn't complicated. It involves invitation and friendship and helping hurting peers. An invitation to be a part of our group or to have a relationship with Jesus can take place in many ways, but it must always be genuine and warm.

What are some key words and phrases that are helpful when reaching out to others?

2. **Learn from the Bible.** Acts 2:42-47 describes the way the early church reached out to the people around them.

What did you learn from the Bible about the nature and importance of outreach?

3. **Keep your outreach simple.** Extending an invitation to another teenager does not have to be complex. The simpler the better. In the early church, outreach was an extension of caring for others, eating together, sharing things, and being friendly toward those who were not yet a part of the community. Jesus talked about being kind to the stranger and helping those in need. These same principles can apply to our outreach.

What are some simple ways we can reach out to others?

4. **Understand why outreach is important.** Outreach involves invitation and friendship, inviting others to be a part of our community and to experience a relationship with Jesus. Our purpose is not to force others to be a part of our community, but to invite them to experience the love and hope we have found.

List some reasons why outreach is important.

5. **Formulate goals and a plan for outreach.** Without goals, we may wander around aimlessly. It's important to have a plan and a purpose behind the ways we reach out to others.

What are the goals our group is trying to reach? How are we going to reach them?

6. **Practice using your outreach skills.** As the saying goes, "Practice makes perfect." In our session we learned many skills and did some role-playing. Being attentive to the needs of others is a great skill to practice. Much of this comes through learning how to listen well.

What are some other important skills you can practice?

Skill Session

Topic: Peer counseling

Supplies: You'll need Bibles, newsprint, a marker, and a photocopy of the "Guidelines for Peer Counseling" handout (p. 42) for each person.

Preparation: Make one photocopy of the "Guidelines for Peer Counseling" handout (p. 42) for each student.

Opener

Have students sit in a circle. Say: **Because we live in a sinful and sometimes evil world, everybody hurts in some manner, and we all need a way to safely deal with our emotions. At one time or another, each of us will be called upon to help a hurting, wounded person. As a part of the body of Christ, we have the privilege to honor Christ by serving one another and others in the midst of emotional chaos. In those situations, we must be completely attentive to other people's needs.**

Today we're going to discuss how to counsel other students when they need a friend to listen, a shoulder to cry on, or more specific help from professionals.

Say: **Before we talk about the practical things we can do to counsel people, let's discuss what the Bible tells us about the importance of counseling.** Assign individual students to read the following passages one at a time, and ask the entire group the questions that follow after the appropriate passage is read.

Genesis 3:16-19:

● **How much responsibility do we share with Adam and Eve for being separated from God? Explain.**

● **What are some contemporary consequences of sin for humanity?**

Matthew 5:13-16:

● **In Jesus' time, what were salt and light used for?**

● **As Christians, how can we function as salt and light in today's society?**

Matthew 22:34-39:

● **When Jesus says, "Love your neighbor," in this passage, who does "neighbor" refer to?**

● **What are some ways you can love your neighbor as yourself?**

Galatians 6:1-5:

● **According to this passage, how are we the same, or different from, the people we help?**

● **What are some ways we can carry each other's burdens?**

● **How can we test our actions?**

Say: **We can use what we just learned in the Bible in virtually every interaction we have with people.**

Ask:

● **What are some specific actions we can take to make ourselves available to help our peers?**

● **If a peer shares intense emotional pain with you, what are some specific ways you can meet his or her needs?**

Understanding the Skills

Have students remain in their circle. Say: **This next activity is designed to strengthen our counseling skills. We can use the acronym SOLER to help us remember the skills. As I explain to you what each letter in the acronym stands for, turn to one of the people next to you and demonstrate the concept I describe.** (SOLER acronym taken from *The Skilled Helper* by Gerard Egan.)

The S stands for "square." When speaking with a person, it's ideal for you to be squarely and directly facing the person.

The O stands for "open." Try to avoid communicating with someone with your arms and/or legs crossed. Having an open posture invites the person you're with to be a part of your life. Crossed arms and/or legs can give a person the impression that you're uninterested, angry, or judgmental.

The L stands for "lean." In a subtle and unobtrusive way, lean your head or torso toward the person sharing. This shows the person that you're attentive to his or her words and you're invested in trying to understand what he or she is saying.

The E stands for "eye contact." By looking at the person instead of the things going on around you, or your watch, or the stain on his or her shirt, you show the person that you're listening to him or her.

The R stands for "relax." In the midst of a deep conversation that may make you feel uncomfortable, it's easy to tense up with your words, body posture, and listening skills. Show the person you're listening to that you're not flustered and you're present in the conversation.

Have each student find one partner and scatter throughout the meeting area. If you have an odd number of students, find a partner of your own. Assign each pair a letter of the SOLER acronym.

Say: **I've just given every pair a letter of the SOLER acronym. With your partner, decide who is going to be number one and who is going to be number two. We're going to do a simple and potentially funny exercise. In this first round, all the number ones will talk. You can talk about anything you want—your dog, school, parents, gravity, weird smells–whatever. The rules are simple. You must never stop talking. You have to talk to your partner for an entire minute.**

If you're a number two, you must do the exact opposite of the letter I assigned you earlier. For example, if I assigned you S, do everything you can to not sit squarely when your partner is talking to you. If I assigned you R, do everything you can to not be and look relaxed.

If there are no questions, begin the activity, and stop the talking time at precisely one minute. After the first round, quickly reassign the acronym letters, and repeat the activity. This time have the number twos share for one minute and have the number ones do the opposite of what their assigned letters are.

When the activity is over, say: **Although this obviously wasn't real life, you may have experienced some of the same feelings people feel when they're talking to you. As we discuss the following questions, try to seriously apply the SOLER acronym when listening to the discussion.** Ask:

● **When you were sharing with your partner, how did your partner's behavior make you feel? What was your reaction?**

● **Why did you react that way?**

● **How are these thoughts and feelings like real-life situations? How are they different?**

● **Which one of these skills do you personally feel like you need to work on?**

● **If you used all these skills in talking with your friends, your teachers, and your parents, how do you think that would affect your relationships with them?**

● **What are ten words that would describe a person who truly communicated this way with everyone he or she came in contact with?** (Encourage words like "compassionate," "attentive," and "focused." Discourage surface-level words like "awesome," "cool," and "nice.") Write the words on a piece of newsprint where everyone can see it.

Say: **The words you came up with describe a person who is caring and loving toward people in need. Those characteristics will draw people to share with you and disclose some very intense thoughts and feelings. Although trust and confidentiality are always top priorities in friendship and in counseling, it's necessary for you to break confidentiality in some situations.** Ask:

● **What are some specific instances when, as a counselor or friend, you must break confidentiality?** (Encourage students to discuss at least the guidelines listed on the "Guidelines for Peer Counseling" handout—when people are in danger of hurting themselves or someone else, when people break the law, or when people are suicidal, for example.)

● **Why is it important to break confidentiality in the situations we named?**

● **If secrets are kept in these situations, what are some possible positive and negative results?**

● **Is it worth the risk to keep confidentiality in such situations?**

Closing

Have students open their Bibles to Philippians 2:1-8. Say: **As we read this passage together, think about how the SOLER acronym can communicate these words to people we're trying to help.**

Have a volunteer read the verses aloud. Then have kids bow their heads and prepare for prayer. Say: **I doubt Jesus needed the SOLER acronym to show people that he cared for them. However, we aren't perfect, and we can hurt others with the smallest actions. Therefore, we must work hard at trying to help the people we care for. As we close, think about what parts of your communication patterns need to be improved. Think about how damaging negative communication can be for someone who is in pain and needs a listening ear. Of the five simple skills we learned about today, pick one you would like God to help you work at and improve. Pray aloud as you feel the need, and I'll close our prayer time together when the time is appropriate.**

Give each person a copy of the "Guidelines for Peer Counseling" handout as the students are leaving, and encourage kids to keep them and refer to them later.

Guidelines for Peer Counseling

When you're helping someone else talk through tough issues, remember the acronym SOLER. Follow these guidelines for active listening:

Square—Sit directly facing the person so he or she knows you're present physically and emotionally.

Open—Open your posture, inviting the person to be a part of your life. Crossed arms and/or legs can give the person the impression that you're uninterested, angry, or judgmental.

Lean—In a subtle and unobtrusive way, lean your head or torso toward the person sharing.

Eye contact—Look at the person so he or she knows you're paying attention to him or her and not what is going on around you.

Relax—Even though you may feel overwhelmed, try to appear relaxed, and have faith that God is with you.

(Source: *The Skilled Helper* by Gerard Egan.)

Confidentiality Guidelines

Don't ever promise to keep a secret that may be harmful to someone. Always report to an adult—such as your pastor or a school counselor—any information you receive that leads you to believe someone is breaking the law or is in danger of hurting self or others.

If you suspect someone is suicidal and you are in no immediate danger of getting hurt, stay with the person until you can send for help and help arrives.

Retreat Plan

Use this retreat plan to help your student leaders understand more about what it means to be Christlike leaders and to discover more about their own leadership gifts and styles.

Retreat Objectives

- Provide spiritual renewal for youth and their adult leaders.
- Assess personal leadership skills and styles.
- Understand the body of Christ and how to function within it.
- Discover that leadership is based in spiritual gifts and that the best leaders work with the whole group to accomplish God's goals.
- Form bonds between youth leaders.
- Commit to imitate Jesus Christ in leadership.
- Voice what leadership is and is not.
- Apply leadership principles to real circumstances.
- Plan and schedule ways to carry out leadership during the year.

Sample Retreat Schedule

Friday
6:00—Sack suppers
7:00—Learning plan 1 and snacks
11:00—Cabin time (Ecclesiastes 4:10-12)
12:00—Lights out

Saturday
8:00—Breakfast
9:00—Personal Bible reading (Romans 12)
9:30—Learning plan 2
11:30—Lunch
12:30—Recreation (See Group Publishing's *On-the-Edge Games for Youth Ministry, Building Community in Youth Groups,* and *Youth Group Trust Builders* for team-building game ideas.)
3:30—Learning plan 3
6:00—Supper
7:00—Leadership planning session and snacks
11:00—Cabin time (Jeremiah 30:21-22 and 2 Corinthians 2:14-15)
12:00—Lights out

Sunday
8:00—Breakfast
9:00—Personal Bible reading (Ephesians 4)
9:30—Closing worship
10:30—Departure

Supplies

You'll need Bibles, pens or pencils, photocopies of the handouts listed in the "Preparation" section, poster board, markers, yarn, newsprint, scissors, paper, masking tape, a box of toothpicks and a bag of marshmallows for every three people, pies, sandwich supplies, cloves, fragrant foods such as oranges and warm brownies, self-hardening clay in several colors (such as Sculpey or Fimo—available in craft stores), monthly calendar pages, and access to an oven.

Preparation

● Make one photocopy of these handouts for each person: "Leadership Pie" (p. 50), "Are You a Jesus-Style Leader?" (pp. 55-56), "Partial Doodle" (p. 58), and "Leadership Opportunities" (p. 61).

● Make one photocopy of the "Leadership Card" handout (p. 47) for each person.

● Cut apart the pieces of each "Leadership Pie" handout (p. 50). Stack each set of pieces separately. When the young people arrive, count out one set per person present, and shuffle the sets together.

● Cut two two-foot-long strips of yarn for each teenager.

● Make one photocopy of the "Ephesians 4 Phrases" handout (p. 53). Cut apart the phrases, and glue each one onto its own index card.

● Cut the "Handful of Leadership Approaches" section off the bottom of each "Leadership Opportunities" handout (p. 61). Cut apart the situations on the "Leadership Opportunities" portion of the handout.

● Write this sentence on chalkboard, poster board, or newsprint: "Leadership is not _____ because _____, but it is _____ because _____."

● Hang large monthly calendar pages on the walls around the room. Pull the bottom of each page up and secure it to the top with tape so that the page is folded in half and no one can see what's written on it.

Learning Plan 1:
Focus on the Body of Christ

Game

Use this game as a transition between sessions, as an introduction to this session, or at any point during the retreat to emphasize that each member of the body of Christ is called to lead.

Give each person a pen or pencil and a photocopy of the "Leadership Card" handout. Have kids form teams according to the last digit of their phone numbers. Then say: **In this game, we'll describe in four ways what it means to be a Christian leader. The first description we'll use is an acronym. Each one of you should write on the top of your handout a three-letter acronym for Christian leadership. For example, the acronym SOS could stand for "says others' strengths," meaning that Christian leaders point out and encourage the strengths in other people. When you've written your acronym and an explanation of what it means, lay your handout in a pile with the rest of your team's handouts.**

When everyone has written an acronym definition, say: **Now choose one acronym—not your own—from your team's pile.** Then ask:

- **What do you like about the definition in your hand?**
- **How will expressing this kind of leadership help our group?**

Have each person find his or her "Leadership Card" handout, and say: **Now write on your handout a silly, serious, or limiting definition of Christian leadership, and give all your handouts to one person on your team. For example, if you were to write a silly definition of leadership, you might write, "Leadership means everybody buys you gifts at Christmas." A serious definition might say, "Leadership means being a servant to others." And an example of a limited definition is "Only adults can be leaders." Each of these definitions can teach us something valuable about what leadership is. For example, my limited definition can help us remember that anyone can be a leader—not just adults.** When students are finished, have one person on each team read each definition aloud while the rest of the team guesses whether it's silly, serious, or limiting, and then names a good thing that definition teaches about leadership.

When each team has discussed its definitions, ask everyone:

- **How can silly definitions help us focus on what's serious about leadership?**
- **How will our group be affected if we take leadership seriously?**
- **What are some ways we tend to limit leadership?**

Say: **Because each Christian is gifted by the Holy Spirit, each Christian is a leader, including each of you. And the church needs you to use your gifts to lead others.**

Leadership Card

1. Write a definition for Christian leadership. This definition must use an acronym (a set of initials such as SOS or ABC) to tell something about leadership.

_____

_____

_____

_____

_____

_____

2. Write another definition for Christian leadership. This definition should be one of the following:

- a silly definition
- a serious definition
- a definition that people use that limits leadership

_____

_____

_____

_____

_____

_____

Learning Activity: Leadership by Gift

NOTE: This book includes a Bible study about spiritual gifts (see pp. 19-21). Young people who have already participated in that Bible study will now have the opportunity to review the information and to talk more about how their gifts impact their leadership.

Give each person seven random pieces from the "Leadership Pie" handouts you cut apart and shuffled earlier. Say: **Trade your seven pieces one at a time without showing what you trade, until you have seven different pieces of pie. You can't request the piece you want, so you'll have to trade many times. In the process, you'll probably memorize most of the seven pieces.**

After a few minutes of trading, invite volunteers to try to name the seven spiritual gifts without looking at the pie pieces. Congratulate students who try to name all seven gifts even if they can't remember all of them.

Have kids trade again, this time with each person trying to get as many of one gift as possible in ninety seconds. After ninety seconds, have volunteers try to name the seven spiritual gifts again.

Say: **The words you traded and memorized are some spiritual gifts, ways to lead in the church. They come from Romans 12:6-8. Every Christian has one of these spiritual gifts, including you. Two other Bible lists of spiritual gifts are in 1 Corinthians 12:27-31 and Ephesians 4:11. Choose the gift you have the most of in your hand and search Romans 12 for ways to lead using that spiritual gift. For example, Romans 12:10 says to honor others above ourselves as a way to lead through the gift of serving.**

For Deeper Study

If your students need more biblical study and background on what each of the spiritual gifts is and how it can be used in the church, you may want to lead them in the Bible study on spiritual gifts in this book (pp. 19-21).

Give each person a piece of paper and markers to record ideas for leadership. If more than one young person is working on the same gift, let kids work together to find ideas.

When kids are finished working, have each person or group share its findings. Then ask:

● **How can the gift you researched contribute to the good of our group?**
● **Why is each way to lead critical to our group?**
● **How can expression of these gifts promote acceptance and unity in our group?**

Pause to pray for the understanding of how to use gifts and the courage to express them to bring good in the group.

Learning Activity: Leadership Pie Assembly

Have each person find someone who collected a different pie piece from what he or she collected. Using ideas from Romans 12, direct pairs to name three ways those two gifts can work together. For example, prophecy and service can work together to "overcome evil with good." When the prophet sees evil and points it out, the servant can find caring ways to help deal with it.

Then have each pair join another pair. Each group of four should find ways their gifts can work together, drawing on ideas from Romans 12.

Finally, have the entire group work together to name ways all seven gifts can work together. Then ask:

● **What would happen in our group if we had only the leadership gift of administration?**

● **What if we had only the gift of mercy?**

● **What if we left out any single gift?**

Have kids form a circle. Guide a time of prayer during which each person contributes a sentence, thanking God for the leader on his or her left.

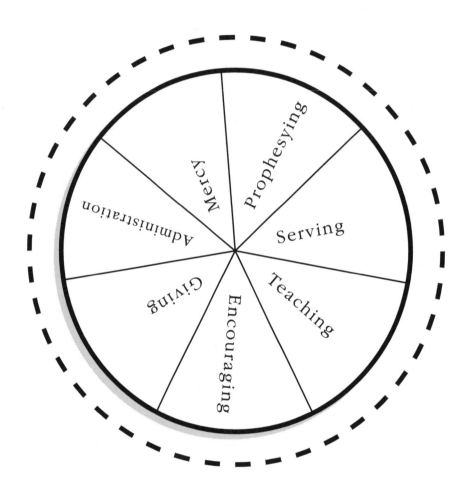

React, Respond, Result

Have kids line up in order of the last four digits of their phone numbers. Then break the line into groups of three, and have each group discuss these questions:

● **We've just discussed the value of each leadership style. When have we been guilty in our group of assuming that one leadership gift is more important than another?**

● **Without naming names, when have you personally been guilty of valuing one leader in our group above another member?**

● **When have you been guilty of failing to add your leadership gift to our group?**

● **How can we encourage each other to lead as God wants us to lead?**

Give each group of three a bag of marshmallows and a box of toothpicks. Instruct each group to compose a structure that shows how God wants leadership expressed in the group.

If young people need ideas as they work, encourage them to think through ways to symbolize these principles: Every person is involved, members encourage each other, the group is both stable and flexible, and all the leadership gifts are represented.

When everyone is finished, have groups share their structures and explain them to one another.

Worship

Direct kids to stay in their groups of three. Give each person a strip of yarn about two feet long, and guide kids to think of their yarn as the leadership God has given them. Invite young people to pray silently as you guide them. Guide the prayer by giving starter sentences like these, directing young people to complete them as they privately talk with God with their eyes closed:

● **God, thank you for giving me a spiritual gift through which to lead in our group. This makes me feel...**

● **One fear I have about leading in our group is...**

● **But others in this group can help me lead because our gifts work together. I've already noticed...**

● **I want to help others lead by...**

● **One more thing I'd like to say is...**

Say: **Now let's worship God together by thanking God for the group. Without each other, we can easily be hurt and broken. Try to break your piece of yarn in half as I read the first segment of Ecclesiastes 4:12: "Though one may be overpowered..."**

Give each person another piece of yarn, and direct the young people in each group to braid their yarn together, each telling the other two why he or she appreciates their leadership. Direct each group to tie a knot at the top and bottom of its braid. Then say: **Now try to break your braid of yarn as I read the rest of Ecclesiastes 4:12: "...two can defend themselves. A cord of three strands is not quickly broken."**

Give each group a pair of scissors. Direct groups to cut their braided yarn into three pieces and then tie knots at the ends of each piece. Then have each person tie one of the braided strips around his or her wrist. Ask:

● **How can this yarn be a tribute to cooperative leadership in our group?**
● **What does it say about the bond we share as leaders?**
● **What does it say about the bond we share with God?**
● **Why do you need the other two in your trio? Why do they need you?**

Invite young people to read Ecclesiastes 4:10-12 aloud and in unison as praise to God for giving them each other. Ask students to keep the yarn on their wrists for at least a week to remind them to encourage each other in leadership.

Snack Idea

Serve pie to remind kids that they are together the body of Christ.

Learning Plan 2:
Leadership That Imitates Christ
Game

Use this game as a transition between sessions, as an introduction to this session, or at any point during the retreat to emphasize leadership that imitates Christ.

Have kids form teams of five. Be sure each team has at least one Bible. Say: **To demonstrate that leadership is something we show, not something we speak, we'll play a game that uses no words. If any artist speaks, that artist's team loses that round, and a point automatically goes to every other team. To play, each team sends to me one member who serves as artist. I'll tell the artists a Bible phrase they need to draw. When I say go, that person runs back to the team to draw the phrase without numbers or words while the rest of you search Ephesians 4 for the phrase. Once any word is guessed, the artist can write that word. The first team to guess the full phrase stands and shouts it. They win a point. Keep your eyes on your Bible to guess accurately!**

Call for an artist from each team to begin the game. Say one of the phrases from Ephesians 4 for all the artists to draw (see the list on page 53). Rotate artists each round so all young people draw an equal number of times. Urge players to keep looking at their Bibles for the answers.

Ephesians 4 Phrases

"Live a life worthy of the calling."

"Be completely humble and gentle."

"Be patient, bearing with one another in love."

"Keep the unity of the Spirit through the bond of peace."

"You were called to one hope."

"Grace has been given as Christ apportioned it."

"Prepare God's people for works of service."

"So that the body of Christ may be built up."

"Until we all reach unity in the faith and in the knowledge of the Son of God and become mature."

"Attaining to the whole measure of the fullness of Christ."

"We will not longer be infants, tossed back and forth."

"Speaking the truth in love."

"We will in all things grow up into him who is the Head, that is, Christ."

"Builds itself up in love, as each part does its work."

"Put off falsehood and speak truthfully."

"In your anger do not sin."

"Work, doing something useful."

"Do not let any unwholesome talk come out of your mouths."

"Get rid of all...brawling and slander, along with every form of malice."

"Be kind and compassionate to one another."

Learning Activity: Leadership Goal Memory

Lead young people in reading Ephesians 4:12-13 aloud together. Then say: **This verse makes a great goal for us as Christian leaders.** Ask:

● **How can we memorize this verse?**

As kids suggest strategies, write them on a piece of newsprint. Then allow kids to vote for their favorite memorization strategy. If students need ideas to get them started, you may want to suggest these possibilities:

● Set it to a rap rhythm.

● Read it repeatedly with a word omitted each time.

● Write one word to a card, scramble the cards, and put them back in order, trying to do it faster each time.

● Write one word to a card and read it, removing a card each time.

When kids have decided on a strategy, spend some time helping them implement that strategy to memorize the verses.

Learning Activity: Individual Leadership Affirmation

Have kids sit in a circle. Be sure each person has a Bible. Ask the youngest person in the group to step inside the circle. Then invite four people in the group to name four different phrases from Ephesians 4 that describe that person's leadership or leadership potential. For example, someone might say, "Sam, you are never afraid to work, doing something useful. Because of your attitude, no one feels like griping."

Continue with the next oldest person, all the way to the oldest.

Learning Activity: Personal Leadership Assessment

Say: **Most people learn how to be leaders by imitating other leaders.** Ask:

● **Why would Jesus be a great leader to imitate?**

● **What qualities of Jesus do you want to imitate in your leadership?**

Give each person a photocopy of the "Are You a Jesus-Style Leader?" handout. Direct kids to move away from each other and fill in their handouts privately.

Give kids several minutes to complete their handouts, and then ask:

● **What did you discover about leadership?**

● **What did you discover about the way Jesus wants you to lead?**

● **How can we help each other develop Jesus-style leadership qualities?**

Invite young people to join you in prayer, asking God to help them become Jesus-style leaders and to look for opportunities to be like Jesus. Then say: **Sometime during this retreat, I encourage you to find some quiet time with God to ask, "How can I shape up my leadership?" Then set some goals for yourself based on God's answers.** Encourage students to take their "Are You a Jesus-Style Leader?" handouts with them to remind them of their goals.

Handout

Are You a Jesus-Style Leader?

Leadership is not standing in front of a crowd to speak or command. Leadership is imitating Christ in attitude and action. Leadership involves three balanced pairs:

- Nurture and correction
- Action and reflection
- Service and prompting

Jesus lived his life in perfect balance. For example, when the woman was caught in adultery, Jesus used both nurture and correction (John 8:1-11).

For each characteristic, rank yourself from one to five, with five being excellent.

Nurture

balances correction

☐ I treat each person as an irreplaceable, one-of-a-kind, cherished creation of God.

☐ When I teach, I begin with what people know and lead them to discover more about Jesus.

☐ I say good things about people—things Jesus would say—even if no one else does.

Correction

balances nurture

☐ I am willing to respond to the corrective words of others rather than get defensive.

☐ I practice and encourage good behavior, knowing that good is more fun than bad. I also recognize that example teaches more than any words.

☐ I talk calmly but directly about negatives that need fixing. I follow God's guidance rather than simply speak my mind.

Action

balances reflection

☐ I practice obedience to God rather than just talk the talk.

☐ I put other people's needs before my own, showing personal care but not allowing others to trample me.

☐ When I enter a room, I look for the person who is standing alone and go talk to that person. If I'm already talking, I open my circle to others.

Reflection

balances action

☐ I take time to listen to Jesus before I speak and act.

☐ I allow myself to be loved and ministered to, rather than do all the giving.

☐ I choose ministry projects based on Jesus' guidance and true need, not just because they will make me look like a good leader.

Service

balances prompting

☐ I look for ways to help with everyday needs like doing chores, helping with homework, and hearing stories of the day.

☐ To help people believe the good that Jesus creates in them, I deliberately point out something good in people every day. This includes complimenting ideas, praising kind actions, and thanking people.

☐ I am willing to do behind-the-scenes work that brings good.

Prompting

balances service

☐ While I serve, I prompt others to turn outside themselves and serve.

☐ I encourage others to make right choices and choose good actions.

☐ I invite others to do good with me, knowing that together we can give each other courage to choose well.

Scoring

1. For each category, add your scores, divide that total number by three, and mark that number on the hexagon.

2. Connect the dots. If you're leading in Christlike balance, you'll see a large, perfect hexagon. If not, you'll see a small or lopsided hexagon.

3. Add up your total score for all categories. If you scored:

61-90—Your leadership tends to be strong and well-balanced. Keep it that way while looking for more Jesus-style characteristics to express.

31-60—You tend to omit Christlike leadership actions. Circle the flat area God wants you to pump up first.

18-30—Your leadership is self-centered, weak, or destructively out of balance. You may be causing damage rather than delight. Don't despair; practice Christlike leadership instead, rereading the quiz questions for ideas.

(adapted from Karen Dockrey, "Are You a Jesus-Style Minister?" GROUP Magazine, January 1993)

React, Respond, Result and Snack Idea

Set out sandwich-making materials. Have kids form groups of three, with three grade levels or age levels represented in each group if possible. Say: **Right now we're going to practice one aspect of leadership—service. I want each of you to make a sandwich for another person in your group of three, so that each person has a sandwich made just the way he or she wants it. Be sure to talk with that person to be sure you make the sandwich the right way.**

When everyone has a sandwich, have kids sit in their groups and eat their sandwiches. As kids eat, have groups discuss these questions:

● **How did you go about finding out the needs of the person you were making a sandwich for?**

● **How can we find out the needs of others so we can serve them according to their needs?**

● **What makes people serve in ways they want to serve rather than in ways others need to be served?**

● **What are some ways we can lead others in our group by serving them?**

Worship

Give each young person a photocopy of the "Partial Doodle" handout and a pen or pencil. Have kids find their own space, and then begin this prayer:

Jesus, we want to imitate you, but sometimes our imitation looks like this doodle. Have kids finish the doodles to match their silent prayers. Continue: **If you drew our leadership the way you wanted it to be, it would look like this.** Have kids add features to their doodles to represent the changes God wants to make in their leadership.

Call for volunteers to tell about their doodles, explaining how God is growing leadership in them. Urge them to keep the doodles in their Bibles as reminders to let God remake them daily into better leaders. Then lead kids in singing several worship songs.

Partial Doodle

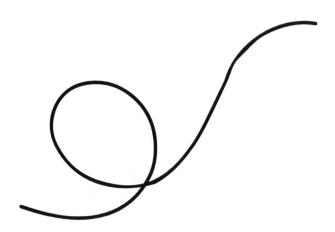

Learning Plan 3:
Mutual Leadership

Game

Use this game as a transition between sessions, as an introduction to this session, or at any point during the retreat to emphasize mutual leadership.

Set up a row of seven chairs for every six people. Enlist three people to be X's and three to be O's seated in the row with the center chair vacant, like the diagram in the margin.

If your group doesn't divide evenly into groups of six, seat an extra two players on the ends and/or play yourself. Explain: **Your goal is to change sides according to these rules:**

- **X's move only to the right.**
- **O's move only to the left.**
- **You can move only one space or jump only one person each move.**
- **You can't have more than one person on a chair at one time.**

When the X's and O's reach an impasse, they start over.

Solution: Keep X's and O's alternated throughout the process. For example, two X's should not be sitting next to each other as the result of a jump, until near the end when sides are almost switched. In the margin is a sample solution showing diagrams of how chairs would look taking sixteen turns to switch.

After the X's and O's have successfully traded places, direct kids to stay in their new seats. Ask:

- **What role did cooperation play in this game?**
- **What would have happened if one person felt that getting to the other side was more important than anyone else getting there?**
- **What can this game teach us about leadership?**
- **How can leaders work together to solve problems?**

Learning Activity:
Leadership Is Not...but Is...

Have kids form a circle. Point to the sentence you wrote on newsprint before the study. Say: **Let's talk about what leadership isn't and what it is. We'll work together to fill in this sentence: "Leadership is not _____ because _____ but is _____ because _____." I'll start with what leadership is and is not, and you fill in the becauses. Then each of you create your own.**

- **Leadership is not bossiness because _____ but is working together because _____.**
- **Leadership is not dominant because _____ but is finding solutions together because _____.**

- Leadership is not giving all the answers in Bible study because _____ but is encouraging the whole group to learn because _____.

- Leadership is not showing favoritism because _____ but is seeing the value of each group member's contribution because _____.

- Leadership is not a few because _____, but it is many because _____.

Say: **Now let's talk about what mutual leadership looks like.**

Learning Activity: Leadership Situations

Have one young person read aloud Jeremiah 30:21-22 while the others follow along. Say: **God draws people close to him and equips them to lead the people near them.** Ask:

- **How has God brought you close to him?**
- **How does closeness to God make you a better leader?**
- **What leadership actions promote closeness between people?**
- **What leadership actions promote closeness to God?**

Say: **It's easier to talk about being a leader among our peers than to actually do it. Let's write about some situations we anticipate facing; then we'll work together to solve them, keeping in mind what God has promised in Jeremiah 30:21-22.** Give each person paper and a pen or pencil. Guide young people to write descriptions of situations they are facing or could face as leaders. Ask them to write one situation per page, and caution them against naming names or including too many details.

As students finish descriptions, ask them to bring them to you. Read through the descriptions to cull out details that are too personal or sensitive. When everyone is finished, have kids form groups of three, with three grade levels or age levels represented in each group. Give each group at least one situation to solve. If you don't have enough situations, include situations from the "Leadership Opportunities" portion of the handout.

Give each person a copy of the "Handful of Leadership Approaches" portion of the handout. Say: **As you work in your groups to solve the situations you've been assigned, each of you should complete the five sentences on the "Handful of Leadership Approaches" handout.**

After several minutes, have groups report how they solved their situations. Then ask:

- **What leadership actions are important when things are going well?**
- **How can leadership help keep small problems from getting bigger?**
- **What steady leadership actions can chisel away at huge problems?**
- **How can mutual leadership affect our ability to solve problems?**

Leadership Opportunities

Situation 1: People are clustering together in age and school groups rather than crossing lines to make friends with the whole group. You want to help people feel more secure and free to make friends with others.

- -

Situation 2: Most adults in your church really like the teenagers and want to get to know them better. You want to help make this happen. But some of the teenagers believe the adults are all talk and no action. And some of the adults think teenagers are too noisy.

- -

Situation 3: The group is taking sides on something. Sarcastic comments are everywhere, but you can't tell what the fight is about. You want to return the group to unity and mutual care.

- -

Situation 4: Two people started a rumor about a third. The three compete heavily for class rank at school. When the third went ahead of the first two, they accused him of cheating. The group is starting to believe it. You want to discourage lying, encourage happiness for others, and yet motivate people to do well in school.

- -

Situation 5: Some people in the group want to elect officers. Others believe this will become a popularity contest and the best leaders won't win. Some say the idea is contrary to gift-based leadership taught in the Bible. They prefer leadership meetings to which everyone is invited.

Handful of Leadership Approaches

Prayer: A sentence prayer for this situation is...

Partnership: I would ask _____ to lead with me in this situation because...

Question: A question I would ask in this situation is...

Action: An action I would take in this situation is...

Gifts: Two spiritual gifts that would work together in this situation are...

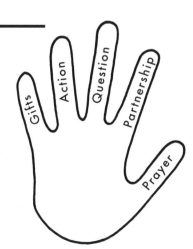

Learning Activity: Leadership "Hand" Out

Say: **The sentences you completed in the last activity represent some important leadership skills.** Have everyone hold up a hand and extend their fingers to memorize the five leadership approaches from the "Handful of Leadership Approaches" handout: prayer, partnership, question, action, and gifts. Say: **These are approaches you can take to solving problems.** Ask:

● **What makes the hand an appropriate symbol for leadership?**

● **How does prayer work like a thumb, partnering with the other four fingers?**

● **How do these approaches incorporate the principles of mutual leadership?**

React, Respond, Result

Have a student read 2 Corinthians 2:14-15 aloud. Say: **God compares the effect we have on people with fragrance. I think we would all agree that smells can be powerful forces. Smells can remind us of someone special or tell us we're close to a farm. Good leadership has a similar effect on people. It serves to remind people of God's presence. And when we work together as leaders, we leave a more complete impression of who God is. Let's tell each other why our leadership smells good!** Have kids get back in their multi-age groups of three. Have each person tell the other two why their actions remind him or her of Jesus. Encourage only positive comments.

Give each young person a clove to remind kids that every action leaves a fragrance or a stench and to choose the former.

Worship

Give each person a lump of self-hardening clay in one of several colors. Be sure you hand out a variety of colors. Say: **In a moment, you'll be forming this clay into a sculpture that represents leadership. You'll take this sculpture home to remind you how God wants you to lead in the year ahead. But first, trade some of your clay with every other person in the room. The mixture of colors will represent mutual leadership.**

When kids are finished with their sculptures, invite volunteers to present their sculptures and talk about what they represent. Then ask:

● **How will you support each other in leadership when we return home?**

● **What's one thing God has taught you about leadership during this retreat?**

- **What do you want people to notice when you return from this retreat?**

Close by praying that kids will work together to remind others of Jesus. Then bake the sculptures while young people eat their snacks.

Snack Idea

Serve fragrant foods such as oranges and warm brownies to remind kids that good leadership reminds people of Jesus. Such leadership includes service and prompting, reflection and action, nurture and correction.

Leadership Planning Session

Say: **Everything we've learned on this retreat means little if we don't put it into practice when we return to our routines. During this session we'll plan for the next year of activity in our group. But first let's do a little dreaming.**

Dream Big

Give each person paper and a marker. Instruct kids to draw or write out their dreams for what the group might become over the next year. Then have kids draw five lines fanning out from each dream. On those lines they should write leadership actions that could help make those dreams come true. For example, a student might draw a picture of a group of students standing in a circle holding hands to symbolize unity. On the lines fanning out from the picture he or she might write, "Welcome new students in a genuine way," "Refuse to gossip," "Focus on the things we have in common," "Be real with each other," and "Encourage each other."

Establish Plans

Say: **Now let's plan some specific opportunities to make our group more like the group of your dreams.** Unfold the calendar pages you hung around the room earlier. Direct kids to write ideas and opportunities on the calendars. Encourage them to be sure their ideas reflect the dreams they have for the group. You may want to share these ideas to get them started:
- education opportunities such as Sunday school and Bible studies
- opportunities for different age levels to interact
- checkup meetings where student leaders work with adults to solve problems and celebrate victories
- opportunities for teenagers to teach and do other ministry in the church as a whole, including training times
- regular meetings for accountability partners
- opportunities for young people to tell each other what they appreciate

The calendar will probably become quite full as students write events on it. Don't discourage people from writing their ideas, but guide kids to find ways to combine opportunities to accomplish more than one purpose at once. For example, affirmation opportunities might come during weekly study sessions.

Take the First Step

When your calendar pages are full, allow young people to claim responsibility for events they would like to help plan and coordinate. Then encourage individuals or teams to spend some time planning steps they'll need to take to make the event a success. Be sure students write down their steps and commit together to take those steps at the right time.

Form Teams

At this time, you may want to have kids form leadership teams for the upcoming year. Two types of teams you might want to establish are family teams and accountability pairs.

Family teams consist of one young person from each grade level represented in the group. Family teams sit together at meetings, contact one another during the week, and check up on each other. You can form these teams within the group of leaders or within the entire youth group. Be sure to add members to the family groups as new young people join your group during the year.

Accountability partners talk weekly to share prayer requests, affirm each other in leadership, encourage each other, and challenge each other.

Closing Worship

Spend some time singing worship songs and giving thanks to God.

Then invite each young person to say one sentence on one of the following subjects, waiting to add a second sentence until each person has said one sentence.

● Thank God for guiding our leadership development.

● Ask for God's wisdom in carrying out our plans, adapting and expanding as God guides.

● Thank God for a new and deeper friendship you've made.

Checkup Sessions

Use these checkup sessions after student leaders are already
exercising their leadership skills. These sessions will give kids
opportunities to support each other and to process issues that
have come up in leadership.

Checkup Session

Scripture: 1 Peter 1:3-7

Supplies: You'll need three different-colored markers for each student, a photocopy of the "Along the Road" handout (p. 68) for each student, and Bibles.

Preparation: Make one photocopy of the "Along the Road" handout (p. 68) for each student.

The Diagnosis

Give each student an "Along the Road" handout and three different-colored markers. Say: **On your handout, I'd like you to use one of the markers to show what your relationship with God was like at each of the points that are listed. So on the line that says "Starting Out," indicate what your relationship with God was like when you first became a Christian or when you first started taking your Christianity seriously. For example, if your relationship with God was going great, put a mark near the line that says "Flyin' Down the Highway." If your relationship with God was horrible, put the mark near "Stuck in a Traffic Jam." Do this for the first four time periods. Please don't go past the "Now" line.**

Have teenagers follow the instructions above two more times. But instead of ranking their relationship with God, have students use a different-colored marker to rank their happiness and another color to rank their relationships with others.

Have each person use the handout to explain to the rest of the group where he or she is right now and how he or she got there. Have the group pray for students who express that they're having a difficult time.

Ask:

● **Do you see any correlation between the three different colors on your handout? Explain.**

● **How have you grown in your faith?**

● **What struggles are you facing now that you didn't have to deal with before?**

The Doctor's Orders

Say: **I'd like you to turn your handout over and write down a statement that describes what effective leadership is for you. For example, if you lead a small group, you might write, "Group members are challenged to seek after God." I'd like you to write it as neatly and elegantly as you possibly can.**

After students write their sentences, say: **Stand up and look at your feet. While continuing to look at your feet, spin around four times as fast as you** can. As soon as you're done spinning, write down your statement just underneath the one you already wrote.

When students finish, ask:

● **How did spinning around affect your ability to write down your statement?**

● **What things make it difficult for us to minister effectively to others?**

● **What things in your life right now are making it difficult for you to effectively minister to others?**

● **What things have you found that help you keep your focus and ability to lead?**

● **What questions do you have about your area of leadership, about God, or about this ministry as a whole?**

● **Are you getting the support you currently need to be an effective leader? Please be completely honest.**

Take as much time as necessary to deal with issues and questions that come up. If your meeting runs over because of questions and discussion, direct students to complete their "Along the Road" handouts at home.

Good Medicine

Say: **I'd like you to complete your "Along the Road" handouts. Remember to use different colors to rank your relationship with God, your happiness, and your relationships with others.**

Ask:

● **Do the marks on your handout go up or down when they get to the future sections? Why?**

Be sure each student has a Bible. Have students form trios to read 1 Peter 1:3-7 and discuss these questions:

● **Look at the low points on your handout. How has God used those times to purify your faith?**

● **What about your future looks hopeful?**

● **What about your future looks bleak?**

● **What keeps you going when times get tough?**

Say: **No matter what your handout looks like now, there is hope for your future. We know that our eternal future is one of bliss and joy with God in heaven. We also know that we have hope right here on earth. God is working on your faith. He is strengthening it and making it pure. He is changing you to be more like Jesus and to be more effective in your ministry efforts.**

Ask:

● **How have you seen God refine your faith?**

Pray: **Lord, thank you for the bright future you have given us. Thank you that you are changing us and refining us. Help us to hold to the hope you have given us in your Son. In Jesus' name, amen.**

Handout
Along the Road

Flyin' Down the Highway

Starting Out

Started in Leadership

One Week Ago

Middle of the Road

Now

One Month From Now

One Year From Now

Five Years From Now

Stuck in a Traffic Jam

Checkup Session

Scripture: Titus 3:4-7

Supplies: You'll need two household items or office supplies for each student leader, self-stick notes, pens or pencils, and Bibles.

Preparation: Gather a wide variety of household items and office supplies. For example, you might collect a wooden spoon, a stapler, a light bulb, a shoe, a pen, a jar, a box of tacks, a book, a sheet of paper, a cheese grater, a glove, paper, and a facial tissue.

Think of an affirmation for each student that is based on who the person is, not what he or she does or looks like. Make sure you connect each affirmation to one of the supplies you bring. For example, you could hold up a facial tissue and say, "(Person's name), you are like this tissue because your heart is soft toward God and others."

The Diagnosis

Set the household items and office supplies in the middle of the room. Have kids sit in a circle around the items.

Say: **I'd like you to find one thing in this pile that you could use to describe how things are going in your area of leadership. The item could symbolize relationships in a group you lead, the difficulties you're facing, the growth of the people you lead, or anything else you'd like to share.**

For example, you might pick up a glove and explain that the leadership you're involved in is like a glove because everyone is working together and fitting into his or her role. Or you could pick up a sheet of paper and explain that the people you lead are like paper cuts because everyone is fighting and hurting each other. As soon as you decide which item best represents your area of leadership, take your turn. When you're finished, put the item down so someone else can use it.

After everyone has taken a turn, ask:

● **Is there anyone here who wasn't able to find an item to symbolize what's going on in your area of leadership? If so, tell us what's going on.**

● **Do you feel that you have a pretty clear idea of how your area of leadership is going? Explain.**

● **What successes have you had since we last met? what difficulties?**

● **What do you enjoy about being a leader?**

● **What aspects of leading are difficult for you?**

Have students repeat the process of using the items for explanation. But this time, have each student find an item that demonstrates how he or she is doing personally.

After each person has shared, take time to pray as a group for those who are struggling. If anyone is having an especially difficult time, ask the person if he or she wouldn't mind talking more with you at the end of the meeting.

Ask:

● **How does your area of ministry affect how you feel about yourself? about God?**

● **To what extent should ministry affect your identity?**

● **If I told you that it was time for you to take a break as a leader, how would it affect the way you feel about yourself? about God?**

Say: **I am *not* going to ask any of you to take a break from leading. But I want you to realize that this ministry is just one of the many things that shape who you are. If you're struggling, it doesn't mean you're an ineffective leader or an ineffective Christian. If you decide to take a break from leading, you're still important and valuable to God, to me, and to this church. God has a plan for your life, and he's using your experiences as a student leader to get you ready for your future.**

The Doctor's Orders

Give each teenager two self-stick notes and a pen or pencil. Say: **On each self-stick note, write down one question you have about something going on in your group, something you don't understand about God, or any other question you might have. You don't have to come up with two questions, but try to come up with at least one. Put your name or initials on each question.**

Have kids stick their notes to a wall in your meeting room. Try to have kids spread the notes out across the wall. Give each teenager three more self-stick notes. Say: **I'd like you to read the questions on the wall. If you feel that you may have an insight or an answer to any of the questions, write it on a self-stick note, and stick your response to the question. Try to respond to at least two questions.**

After all the teenagers have given their answers, say: **Please retrieve your original questions and the responses attached to them. If one of your questions doesn't have any responses attached to it, please give it to me.**

Give students a few minutes to retrieve their questions and read the responses. With the entire group, address the questions that didn't have any responses. Then ask students to share discoveries they made, insights they had, and questions they need more help with. Take as much time as necessary to address every question students have.

Good Medicine

Thank students for their insights and questions. Instruct students to sit around the supplies you used in "The Diagnosis" activity. Have teenagers open their Bibles and follow along as you read Titus 3:4-7 aloud.

Say: **I'm thankful for the work you do for your peers, for me, and for God. But I really want you to understand that God's love for you is not wrapped up in what you do. He has saved you and called you his own simply because he loves you. It's wonderful that you express your faith by serving others. However, God loves you for who you are, and so do I.**

Use the supplies in the pile to tell each student one thing you especially appreciate about him or her. Make sure your affirmation is connected to who the person is and not what he or she does or looks like. For example, you could hold up a facial tissue and say, "(Person's name), you are like this tissue because your heart is soft toward God and others." Or you might hold up a flashlight and say, "(Person's name), you are like this flashlight because you help bring light to unclear situations."

If you don't have time to do this with each student, have students form pairs and affirm each other in the manner described above.

Checkup Session

Scripture: 1 Samuel 16:1, 6-7

Supplies: You'll need slips of paper, felt-tip pens, a roll of toilet paper, sheets of paper, pens or pencils, and Bibles.

Preparation: On a slip of paper write, "an Olympic sprinter, a doctor, and a mother." On another slip of paper write, "a race-car driver, a ten-year-old, and a pastor." On a third slip of paper write, "a pilot, a pizza delivery person, and a high school athlete."

The Diagnosis

Have students form three groups. Give each group one of the slips of paper you prepared before the study. Say: **With the members of your group, I'd like you to decide how each person on your slip of paper defines success. For example, if your slip of paper said, "high school athlete," you might decide that person defines success as being voted all-league or all-city.**

When groups finish, ask:

● **How do most people define success?**

● **How do most people define success in ministry?**

● **How do you define success in the areas of ministry you're currently involved in?**

● **Based on that definition, do you feel that you currently are successful or unsuccessful in ministry?**

Have each person in the group share about his or her area of ministry by telling others what is and isn't going well. Encourage others to offer their support and insights to the person who is sharing. Then have students form pairs to pray together for God's help and direction in their responsibilities.

The Doctor's Orders

Give each student a felt-tip pen. Have students form a straight line and then sit down. Roll out the toilet paper next to the line. Say: **I'd like you to write down on the toilet paper any questions you have about your area of leadership, the people you're serving, our ministry or church, upcoming events, or God. Please write one question on each square. You may use up to three squares, and you must use at least one square.**

When everyone is finished, roll the toilet paper back up, and have the teenagers sit in a circle. Rip the first question off the roll, read it aloud, and give the best answer you can. Invite students to offer their opinions and insights regarding the question.

Say: **We're going to pass the toilet paper around the circle. When the roll comes to you, rip off the first square, read the question aloud, and then give the best answer you can come up with. After you've answered the question, anyone in the group is welcome to add to your answer. After the question has been addressed, pass the roll to the person on your right.**

Pass the roll to the person on your right to begin the question-and-answer time. After all the questions have been answered, say: **Thanks so much for your questions and wisdom. If you have any more questions, please stay after this meeting and talk with me.**

Good Medicine

Have teenagers form groups of three. Give each group a sheet of paper and a pen or pencil. Then have groups discuss these questions:

- **Read 1 Samuel 16:1, 6-7. What are the "outward" things of ministry?**
- **What are the inward aspects or the "heart" things of ministry?**
- **What aspects of ministry are important to God? to you?**

Say: **Draw a line down the middle of your sheet of paper. On one side of the line, list all the things that are necessary for each person's area of ministry to *appear* successful. On the other side of the paper write down all the things that are necessary for each person's area of ministry to *actually be* successful. As you work on that side of your list, think about what God wants from you and what his goal is for your area of ministry.**

Have each trio share its list. Then say: **Many people think numbers are the most important indicators of success. Large groups and growing numbers can indicate that a group is healthy. However, numbers don't necessarily indicate success. I think success is found in spiritual growth. Have you grown in your faith? in your leadership abilities? Has one person come closer to God or gained a more accurate understanding of who God is through your leadership? If so, you have been successful. Goals are important and vision is essential. But remember the real goal of what we do—we are working for changed lives.**

Checkup Session

Scripture: Romans 8:28-32

Supplies: You'll need an apple, a few plastic knives, a plate, paper, pens or pencils, and Bibles.

Preparation: Wash the apple.

The Diagnosis

Have students sit in a circle. Put an apple and a few plastic knives on a plate in the middle of the circle. Say: **Imagine this apple symbolizes the ministry you're involved in right now. Think about the things that make you frustrated, discouraged, or tired of being in leadership. As soon as you think of something, pick up the apple, and cut out a chunk with one of the knives. As you cut out the chunk, explain to the rest of the group what your chunk symbolizes. Then put down the apple, and hold on to your chunk.**

Allow each person to share. After each student shares, encourage discussion by asking questions like these:

- **How many of you have faced a similar circumstance?**
- **How did you deal with it?**
- **How would you deal with this situation if it happened to you?**

After everyone has had a chance to share, ask:

- **How is what happened to the apple like what frustrations and discouraging circumstances do to the ministry you're involved in? How is it different?**
- **How is what happened like what frustrations and discouraging circumstances in ministry do to _you?_ How is it different?**
- **What can you do to avoid being overwhelmed and torn apart by the frustrations involved with leadership?**

Instruct students to set aside their apple chunks to eat later in the meeting.

The Doctor's Orders

Have students form groups of three. Say: **I'd like each person in your group to discuss any questions or problems he or she has encountered since the last time we met. As a group, brainstorm about ways to answer or deal with the issue. Then pray for each person in the group concerning his or her problem or question. After everyone has had an opportunity to share, I'd like your group to choose one question or problem to bring before the other student leaders.**

Give groups about fifteen minutes to talk and pray. Then give each group a few sheets of paper and a pen or pencil, and say: **I'd like each group to bring its problem or question before the other groups. After the issue has been raised, I'd like each group to come up with a solution, principle, or insight regarding the question or problem. However, your solution must be in the form of an acronym. An acronym is a word formed from the first letters of several words. For example, "KISS" is an acronym for "Keep it simple, stupid."**

Your group's acronym can be humorous or straightforward. You'll have about three minutes to prepare it; then all the groups will share their acronyms.

Have each group share its question or problem; then direct groups to come up with their acronyms. Have groups share the acronyms they came up with while encouraging them to offer the insights and thoughts they had while they created their acronyms. Create your own acronym for each question, and share it along with the student groups.

After each group has shared its question or problem, say: **You've raised some excellent questions and come up with some excellent answers. Does anyone else have any questions that need to be addressed before we move on?**

Spend as much time as necessary discussing questions that students raise. If you run out of time, have students complete the "Good Medicine" activity individually instead of with partners.

Good Medicine

Have students form pairs. Ask pairs to read Romans 8:28-32 aloud. Ask:
● **How have you seen God bring good out of difficult circumstances in your life?**
● **How would you be different if you never had to face difficult circumstances?**

Say: **I'd like you to think about the chunk of apple you cut off at the beginning of this meeting. With your partner, try to think of one way God could use the situation you described to the group to accomplish good in your life. As soon as you think of how the situation can be used for good, eat your chunk of apple as a sign of thanksgiving for God's plan for your life.**

After pairs share, close the meeting in prayer, thanking God for working out his plan in everything we face.

Checkup Session

Scripture: Psalm 89:1-8

Supplies: You'll need 16-gauge copper wire, wire cutters, string, scissors, tape, one uninflated balloon for each person, felt-tip markers, newsprint, slips of paper, pens or pencils, and a Bible.

Preparation: Cut a four-inch length of wire for each person. Cut one piece of string for each person. Each piece of string should be long enough to stretch from the ceiling to the top of your students' heads while they're sitting. Tape the pieces of string to the ceiling.

The Diagnosis

Have students form a circle, and give each person one uninflated balloon.

Say: **Sometimes being a leader is stressful. Let's take some time to talk about various aspects of leadership that have stressed us out recently. I'd like you to blow up your balloon, tie it off, and then write on it one thing that is causing stress for you right now. That issue can be either personal or related to your role as a leader.**

As kids are blowing up their balloons, make soft-tip markers available. When students are finished writing on their balloons, say: **Find a partner, and talk about the stress you've described on your balloon. When you've done that, tie your balloon to a string hanging from the ceiling.** Give students five minutes to talk about their stress and tie their balloons to the pieces of string. Then ask volunteers to share about the stress they described on their balloons.

Then ask:

● **How did it feel to share your stress with your partner? Why?**

● **Which area of your life is your stress coming from—leadership or your personal life? Why do you think that is?**

● **Have you ever felt like stress was hanging over your head, waiting to crush you?**

● **What were you thinking about as you listened to your partner's stress?**

● **How can we help you deal with your stress?**

The Doctor's Orders

Say: **Stress can wear away at our ability to lead others—and if we don't deal with it properly, it can damage our relationship with God. I'd like us to examine what stress looks like.**

Give one piece of wire to each student. Say: **When stress enters our lives, it** has a tendency to bend us out of shape. To symbolize that, make a ninety-degree bend in your wire.** When students have done this, continue: **Then when more stress comes along, it bends us further. Bend your wire another ninety degrees—so that both ends are touching.** Say: **Now I'd like you to simulate what a lot of stress can do. Unbend your wire and then bend it again in the same place. Do this again and again as fast as you can.** Give kids a few seconds to do this. Encourage kids to do this very quickly.

Say: **OK, stop. You'll probably notice that one of two things has happened. Either your wire got very warm at the spot where you bent it, or your wire broke. This is a great example of what stress can do to us. If we don't deal appropriately with stress, it can "heat up" our lives and even break us. The best way to keep stress from breaking us is to find ways to manage it.**

Ask students to brainstorm about stress-management ideas. For example, students might say, "Take a nap," "Exercise," or "Talk to a friend." As students are brainstorming, have a volunteer write their ideas on a piece of newsprint taped to the wall. When they've listed several ideas, thank students for sharing their ideas.

Distribute slips of paper and pens or pencils. Set out tape where everyone can use it. Say: **I'd like you to pick out one or two stress-management ideas that you might use and write them on your slip of paper. When you've done that, tape your paper to a piece of wire.**

When everyone is finished, ask each person to find his or her own space in the room.

Say: **Picking your stress reliever is a good step. However, it's even better to think of some ways to use it. I'd like you to think about what's happening in your life right now, and come up with some ways you can use the stress reliever.**

Allow students two minutes to think of ways to relieve stress in their lives. When everyone is finished, call students back together, and ask volunteers to share some of the stress-relieving ways they thought of. Say: **Now that you've thought about ways to use it, I'd like you to make a public commitment to using this stress reliever in your life. I'd like you to use your stress reliever to pop the balloon you hung from the ceiling earlier.**

Give students time to find their balloons and pop them with their wires.

Good Medicine

Say: **Here's the good news! Jesus wants us to live lives free from stress. In fact, he loves us so much that he wants us to cast all our cares on him— even difficult, stressful problems!**

Read Psalm 89:1-8 to your group. Say: **God is faithful to help us deal with the stress we encounter—all we have to do is ask. Before we leave, I want to double-check and find out what issues you're facing in your roles as leaders.**

What do we need to talk about today that we haven't discussed yet?

Give students a few minutes to voice concerns and ideas. Make sure you carefully listen to each issue and address it as needed. You may want to make yourself available afterward to talk with students who want to discuss further issues they're facing.

Close with a prayer, asking God to help students when they become burdened with stress.

Basic Training Activities

Use these basic training activities to give kids a basic understanding of important aspects of leadership. Use these activities throughout your leadership training program in partnership with other activities—at the end of a Bible study or a Skill Session, for example. Or you may want to use them by themselves in short meetings.

Basic Training

Topic: Communication skills

Supplies: You'll need scissors, photocopies of the "Nonverbal Listening" handout (p. 82) and photocopies of the "Communication Skills" handout (p. 82).

Preparation: For each pair of students, make one photocopy of the "Nonverbal Listening" handout (p. 82), and cut the sets of messages apart. Make one photocopy of the "Communication Skills" handout (p. 82) for each student.

Understanding the Basics

Say: **Effective leadership requires the ability to communicate effectively. The exchange of information or messages between a sender and a receiver is more complicated than it looks at first glance. Since as much as 93 percent of information we receive is communicated through nonverbal behavior (Harvey A. Robbins, Ph.D., *How to Speak and Listen Effectively*), we'll begin with a quick exercise in sending and receiving nonverbal messages.**

Have students form pairs. Give one person in each pair the "Nonverbal Messages 1" section of the handout and the other person the "Nonverbal Messages 2" section. Have one person demonstrate the first nonverbal facial and body posture while the other person is talking (suggested topics might be "my dream date," "my dream vacation," or "my dream family"). As soon as the person talking can identify the nonverbal clue the other person is sending, partners should switch roles. Have pairs do this until each person has demonstrated all three of his or her nonverbal messages.

Applying the Skill

Give each person a photocopy of the "Communication Skills" handout. Ask students to read their handouts. Then ask them:
- **Which role do you prefer: sender or receiver?**
- **Why did you choose the role you did?**
- **In what way will paying attention to your receiver's nonverbals increase your effectiveness as a communicator?**
- **In what ways did Jesus apply these communication principles during his ministry on earth?**

Putting It Into Practice

Say: **Please take these handouts with you, and refer to them as you need to in your leadership role. Let's try to apply these skills in a variation of a familiar game.**

Have students form a circle. If you have a large group, have students form groups of ten to fifteen people and then form circles. Tell students they'll be playing the Telephone Game but will be racing to move two different messages around the circle at the same time. One message will move clockwise around the circle, and the other message will move counterclockwise around the circle.

Start this message with one person, and have each person *whisper* it, in a clockwise direction, to the person sitting next to him or her: "Clockwise speakers always finish at least two minutes earlier than the deadline." Start this message with the person sitting to the right of the first messenger so it moves around the circle in the opposite direction: "Counterclockwise listeners always pay attention to the last two minutes before the deadline."

When students have finished playing the game, ask the following questions:

● **Why was it so difficult to pass the message without any errors?**

● **Why is it so important as leaders to make sure the message is properly received and understood?**

● **When has a miscommunicated message caused problems for a group you were a part of?**

Say: **As you can see, communication skills are a very important part of being an effective student leader. I encourage you to develop and practice these skills in your everyday lives.**

Nonverbal Listening

Nonverbal Messages 1

1. I'm bored with what you're saying, and I'd rather be home cleaning my room.
2. I'm angry with you, and I'm ready to debate.
3. I'm excited about what you're telling me, and I want to join you.

Nonverbal Messages 2

1. I'm frustrated that you keep on talking without giving me a chance to say anything.
2. I'm distracted by the attractive person behind you, and I'm not really listening to what you're saying.
3. I'm listening carefully, and I empathize with what you're saying.

Communication Skills

Sender

● Prepare.
● Love and pray for others.
● Pay attention to your receiver's nonverbal behavior.
● Especially in a peer leadership situation, communicate clearly upfront your role and responsibility. Serve, don't boss!

Message

● Keep it simple.
● Use a variety of visual aids such as handouts or overhead transparencies.
● Use active experiential learning: Avoid lecture and encourage discussion and application.

Receiver

● Listen well: Maintain eye contact, smile, lean toward the speaker, focus on the message, and reflect or paraphrase the message back to the sender.
● Love and respect the sender.
● Ask questions.
● Provide positive feedback and appreciation.

Basic Training

Topic: Role modeling

Supplies: You'll need photocopies of the "Role Model" handout (pp. 85-86), one large dinner roll for each person, toothpicks, and markers.

Preparation: Before the session, make one photocopy of the "Role Model" handout (pp. 85-86) for each student.

Understanding the Basics

Have students sit in a circle. Give each person a dinner roll and several toothpicks. Make markers available to everyone. Say: **Today we're going to talk about an essential leadership quality. Before I tell you exactly what we're going to talk about, let's take some time to get to know each other better. I'd like you to make a small replica of yourself using the materials I've given you. As you make your little person, think of traits and attitudes you've gained from someone else. If you can, include those in your little person. If you can't think of a way to highlight them, just remember them.**

Give students three minutes to work at creating their people. When they're finished, have kids form groups of three and present their creations. Then ask:

- **What traits did you include or think of as you created?**
- **How were these traits passed on to you?**
- **Do you look up to the person you got those traits from? Why?**

Say: **Role modeling is an essential element of leadership in two ways: We have to set an example and follow the examples others set. Let's spend some time looking at these two sides of role modeling.**

Applying the Skill

Give each person a copy of the "Role Model" handout. Ask students to fold their handouts in half and briefly look over the chart on the top half. Then ask students to stand. Designate one corner of the room for people who are interested in being role models. Designate another corner of the room for people who are looking for role models. Say: **Because the concept of role modeling involves two very different aspects, I'd like you to focus on the aspect you feel you need right now.**

Allow students time to gather in the corners of their choice. Once they're there, have each person pick one of the four qualities listed on the section of the handout and discuss his or her reasons for choosing that quality as an important focus for either choosing or being a role model. When students are finished, ask volunteers to share their choices.

Say: **Whether you feel like you need to find a role model or you desire to work on your skills as a role model, the most important thing to remember is that God's Word holds the key for you.**

Gather students together, and direct them to look briefly at the "Biblical Role Models" section of their handouts. Say: **The secret to being a role model involves two parts: (1) knowing about great examples in God's Word and (2) understanding why these people are good role models.**

Have students form groups of four, and assign each group a different role model from the "Biblical Role Models" part of the handout. (It's OK to assign a role model to more than one group). Give groups three minutes to prepare sixty-second role-plays about how their biblical role models might handle modern-day situations. The situations should be based on the information on the handout.

After three minutes, have groups name their characters and present their role-plays. As groups make their presentations, ask the audience to look for key elements that made these people role models. After each role-play, ask:

● **What made this person a role model?**

● **Which traits would you like to add to your lifestyle? Why?**

● **How can you be the same type of role model as this person?**

Say: **The Bible isn't the only place to find good examples of role models. As leaders, it's important to *look* for role models and to *be* role models.**

Putting It Into Practice

Have students form pairs. If possible, pair up students who are looking for role models with students who want to be role models. Ask pairs to spend a few minutes reviewing their handouts. Then ask each person to commit to developing one trait over the next two weeks. For example, a student looking for a role model might commit to looking for someone who knows God's Word.

In pairs, have kids discuss initial concerns and prayer requests related to role modeling. Then ask students to close in prayer for each other. Remind kids to take their handouts with them to use in finding and being role models.

Handout
Role Model

Choose a Role Model

- Someone who lives life by God's standards.
- Someone who demonstrates God's love.
- Someone who knows God's Word.
- Someone who responds to God's call.

Be a Role Model

- How can I live by God's standards?
- How can I demonstrate God's love?
- How can I know God's Word better?
- Where is God calling me?

Biblical Role Models

Paul's nephew stood for the right thing (Acts 23:12-22).

Paul's nephew heard about a plot to kill Paul. The nephew told Paul, who immediately called a centurion to take his nephew to report to the commander in charge. The result? Paul was saved.

Caleb and Joshua followed God wholeheartedly (Numbers 14:5-9).

The Israelites had come to the edge of the land that God had promised them. However, they were afraid to enter it until they were sure it was safe. God asked Moses to send Caleb and eleven other men to scout out the territory. Caleb (along with Joshua) trusted God's strength to conquer the inhabitants of the land God had promised.

Jael was fearless (Judges 4:17-24).

Jael, a supporter of the Israelites, was a desert dweller who knew all about the battle going on between Israel and the King of Canaan. Israel overtook Canaan and the king fled to Jael's tent to hide. Jael gave the king something to drink, told him to rest, and promised protection. While the king was sleeping, she drove a tent peg through his temple.

Ezra taught God's Law (Ezra 7:10).

Ezra studied and taught Scripture. He was very well-respected. In fact, the king granted him everything he ever asked for. The Bible says, "The hand of the Lord his God was upon him" (Ezra 7:6b). Ezra was loved by many. His teachings were sought after. But Ezra was a role model because he lived what he taught.

Phoebe served the church (Romans 16:1-2).

Phoebe lived in the port city of Cenchrea, which was about six miles east of Corinth. Many people came and went from her town, including Paul the apostle. She served and ministered and helped people in the church.

Gaius was faithful to the truth (3 John 1-6).

Gaius was a church leader. When missionaries came into town, Gaius faithfully stood by them and provided for their needs. His actions became so well-known that John wrote him a personal note and called Gaius his dear friend. Even though his actions might have caused him to be kicked out of the church, he remained faithful.

Basic Training

Topic: Decision making

Supplies: You'll need photocopies of the "Oodles of Options" handout (p. 89), photocopies of the "Questions and Answers for Decision Makers" handout (p. 90), paper, pens or pencils, newsprint, and a marker.

Preparation: Make three photocopies of the "Oodles of Options" handout (p. 89). Make one photocopy of the "Questions and Answers for Decision Makers" handout (p. 90) for each person.

Understanding the Basics

Say: **Leadership requires the ability to make decisions. Learning to make decisions is a maturational process because it forces us to take responsibility for ourselves. When faced with a decision, we need to ask ourselves three critical questions: "What do I want to accomplish in the long run?" "What are my options in this situation?" and "What immediate course of action should I take?"**

As you distribute a piece of paper and a pen or pencil to each student, ask if anyone knows what a mission statement is. Say: **A mission statement summarizes what you believe to be your main purpose. Companies sometimes create mission statements to define what they intend to provide and how they plan to provide it. I'd like you to take a few minutes to think about your life and write down your own personal mission statement. If possible, keep your statement to one or two sentences. For example, you might write, "My life mission is to seek and follow God's leading in my life. I will pursue excellence in everything I do so I will be prepared to take the responsibilities God gives me in the future."**

After a few minutes, ask volunteers to read aloud their mission statements. Then say: **When you know what your mission in life is, you're better able to make decisions. That's because our actions are directed by our goals, and we make decisions—consciously or unconsciously—to achieve those goals. Identifying your mission or purpose in life helps answer the question, "What do I want to accomplish in the long run?"**

Applying the Skill

Have kids form three groups. Assign each group a different scenario from the "Oodles of Options" handout. Ask each group to read its scenario and write some options on the handout. After a few minutes, have each group give its handout to

Good advice

- doesn't try to control people or situations; isn't self-serving.
- may keep you out of danger.
- makes you feel comfortable with the decision you've made.

Bad advice

- tries to control other people or situations for the person's own benefit.
- may put you in danger.
- may make you question whether you've done the right thing.

another group, which will then list the pros and cons for each option. After a few more minutes, have groups give their handouts to the other group, which will then have three minutes to discuss and select the "best" option.

Say: **Decision making requires that you identify your options and choose from among them. Sometimes it can be difficult to choose.** Ask:

- **When you're struggling with a choice, where can you turn for guidance?**
- **How can you tell the difference between good and bad advice?**

To get kids started, you might want to share some of the ideas in the box in the margin. As kids respond, write their ideas on a piece of newsprint under columns labeled "Good Advice" and "Bad Advice." Encourage kids to make note of some of the responses themselves.

Putting It Into Practice

Say: **The action you take after making a decision shows how committed you are to that decision. To not act on a decision is as ineffective as never reaching a decision at all. If you have trouble following through even after you've chosen a particular option, it can be helpful to practice what's been called "advance decision making."**

Imagine, for example, that you've been meeting regularly with a group of students to prepare for your college entrance exams, and this Thursday night the group is going to review your least favorite subject. To complicate matters, someone you really like has invited you to a party that night. What will you do?

Encourage discussion, and then say: **Those of you who would choose to attend the study session rather than the party would be acting on a decision you made in advance. You would have decided, long before this new option presented itself, that you were going to do whatever it took to increase your chances of getting into college. Deciding something in advance sometimes makes it easier to stay committed to your mission and to act accordingly.**

Now in your three groups, come up with some other examples of advance decision making. I'll give you five minutes to come up with a short scenario that your group will act out for the rest of the class.

After five minutes, have each group perform its scenario. After each performance, ask students to identify what decisions were made in advance.

Give each person a copy of the "Questions and Answers for Decision Makers" handout. Encourage students to keep their handouts for future reference.

Handout
Oodles of Options

Scenario 1—You've been dating someone who's very popular, and everyone at school seems to envy you. But lately, that person has done some things that bother you, and you've become attracted to someone very quiet who attends another school. What do you do?

Scenario 2—You've saved up for a trip to the beach, but one week before you're supposed to go, you learn that you need to replace the transmission in your car. The mechanic says the transmission could last a few more months or could cause your car to break down any minute. You can't afford to replace it *and* go to the beach. What do you do?

Scenario 3—You think you want to be a lawyer, and now it's time to decide which college to attend. You've applied to the one you like the best (a liberal arts college), but you haven't heard from them. Meanwhile, another school known for its engineering and agriculture programs has offered you a full scholarship. You've already been accepted to a community college that offers degrees in both liberal arts and technical fields. What do you do?

Handout
Questions and Answers
for Decision Makers

- What do I want to accomplish in the long run?
- What are my options in this situation?
- What immediate course of action should I take?

"You guide me with your counsel" (Psalm 73:24a).

"My flesh and my heart may fail, but God is the strength of my heart and my portion forever" (Psalm 73:26).

"Trust in the Lord with all your heart and lean not on your own understanding; in all your ways acknowledge him, and he will make your paths straight" (Proverbs 3:5-6).

"But wisdom is proved right by her actions" (Matthew 11:19b).

"If any of you lacks wisdom, he should ask God, who gives generously to all without finding fault, and it will be given to him" (James 1:5).

Basic Training

Topic: Delegating

Supplies: You'll need photocopies of the "Power to the People" handout (p. 93), and three quarters for each person.

Preparation: Make one photocopy of the "Power to the People" handout (p. 93) for each student. Practice spinning a quarter according to the directions in the "Understanding the Basics" activity.

Understanding the Basics

Have students sit or stand around a table with you. If you don't have a table large enough for your group, sit with your students in a circle on a wood or tile floor. Hold a quarter on its edge by resting the bottom of the quarter on the table and holding the top of the quarter with your index finger. Flick the side of the quarter with your other index finger so that the quarter spins on the table like a top. If the quarter doesn't spin, pick it up and try again.

As the quarter is spinning, say: **This quarter represents a responsibility in ministry. Let's say it stands for leading worship. Don't let this quarter fall off the table. If it stops spinning near you, pick it up and get it spinning again.**

While your students keep the quarter spinning, spin another quarter on the table. Instruct students to keep both quarters on the table and to make sure the quarters keep spinning. Say: **This quarter stands for the handouts that need to be photocopied before a meeting.**

Keep adding quarters and explaining what each quarter stands for until it's impossible for your group to keep all the quarters spinning on the table.

Say: **Imagine how difficult it would be for me to keep these quarters spinning if you weren't here. I would be completely overwhelmed, and there would be no way for me to keep everything going. I am so thankful for all that you do to help.**

Ask:

● **In your area of leadership, what are some of the "spinning quarters" or responsibilities you deal with?**

● **Are you able to handle those responsibilities right now? Why or why not?**

Applying the Skill

Say: **As a leader, one of your most important responsibilities is delegation. Delegation makes ministry more enjoyable and manageable for you. Delegating also gives others an opportunity to use and exercise the gifts** they've been given. For example, if I decided I was the only one who knew how to lead and student leadership was over, how would you grow in your leadership skills? How would you fulfill the calling God has given you? When you delegate responsibilities, you aren't slacking or being lazy. You're investing in other leaders.

Ask:

● **What areas of your leadership could you delegate to someone else?**

● **What areas of your leadership absolutely must be done by you?**

● **What's the difference between delegating responsibility and ordering others around?**

● **What potential problems do you see that may come with delegating?**

● **How do you decide what you should delegate and to whom?**

Have teenagers form pairs. Give every person a copy of the "Power to the People" handout. Say: **When Moses served as judge over the people of Israel, he became overworked and overwhelmed with all his responsibilities. Moses' father-in-law, Jethro, urged Moses to delegate responsibility to others. This handout shows how Moses decided who he should give responsibilities to.**

Think of one important responsibility related to your area of leadership that should be delegated. With your partner, use the guidelines on the handout to determine who would be a good person to ask for help. Then talk about how you would go about delegating that task to that person.

Putting It Into Practice

After several minutes, say: **Jethro also encouraged Moses to train the people he chose to delegate responsibility to. As leaders, it's essential for us to train and support the people we delegate to. So when someone agrees to take on responsibility, it's important that you offer suggestions as to how it can be done. You should also periodically check up on the person to make sure the responsibility isn't overwhelming or frustrating the person.**

With your partner, I'd like you to discuss what kind of training and support you'll offer to the person or people you discussed while using the handout.

Ask:

● **Do you feel that you have the knowledge to train and support the person you have chosen to delegate responsibility to?**

● **What support and training do you need to effectively complete your responsibilities as a student leader?**

Say: **If a person declines a responsibility you offer him or her, try not to be disappointed or offended. And don't avoid including that person in other responsibilities. Be patient with the people you lead as you invest in them.**

Encourage your students to take the handouts home for future reference and to read all of Exodus 18. Then ask one of your students to close the meeting in prayer.

Following Moses'
Example of Delegating

Moses gave responsibility to people who...

feared (or revered) God.   Exodus 18:21

were trustworthy.   Exodus 18:21

were honest.   Exodus 18:21

were capable.   Exodus 18:25

knew their own limitations.   Exodus 18:26

Before delegating an important responsibility, ask yourself the following questions:

● What is the person's commitment level?

● How has the person handled other responsibilities?

● What are the person's gifts and strengths?

● Does the person have time to or want to help out?

● How can I help this person grow in his or her ability to lead and serve?

Basic Training

Topic: Group dynamics

Supplies: You'll need photocopies of the "Group Dynamics" handout (p. 95), photocopies of the "Group Case Studies" handout (p. 96), paper, and pens or pencils.

Preparation: Make one photocopy of the "Group Dynamics" handout (p. 95) and one photocopy of the "Group Case Studies" handout (p. 96) for each student.

Understanding the Basics

Give each person paper and a pen or pencil. Encourage each student to reflect on the best group experience he or she has had and write at least three reasons why that experience was the best. Then have kids form groups of three to share their experiences and reasons.

After a few minutes of discussion, say: **As you may have discovered, the success of group experiences has a lot to do with the way people treat each other. Let's talk about some characteristics of an effective group.**

Applying the Skill

Give each person a photocopy of the "Group Dynamics" handout. Say: **Look through your handout for group characteristics you just discussed.**

After several moments, ask:

● **What's an experience you discussed in your group that illustrates one of the characteristics on this handout?**

● **What differences will it make in your group of students if you practice these characteristics of leadership?**

Putting It Into Practice

Have kids form groups of five to seven. Give each group a copy of the "Group Case Studies" handout, and assign one case study to each group. Say: **In your group, discuss the case study I've assigned you. Talk about ways the student leader in the situation could effectively handle the group-dynamic situation.**

After several minutes of discussion, ask each group to describe its case study and the strategies it came up with. Then say: **I encourage you to develop and practice these communication skills in your everyday life.**

Encourage students to take their "Group Dynamics" handouts with them and refer to them as they prepare for their student leadership responsibilities.

Group Dynamics

Role of the Group

- To accomplish more than any one person could (Ecclesiastes 4:9-12).
- To encourage one another (1 Thessalonians 5:11).
- To hold each other accountable (James 5:16).
- To be united in order to glorify God (Romans 15:5-6).

Roles Within the Group

Leaders

- To lead with humility and servanthood (Philippians 2:1-18).
- To develop a strong relationship with God (2 Corinthians 13:5).
- To nurture other Christians in their faith (John 21:17; Deuteronomy 8:3).
- To equip group members to do ministry (Ephesians 4:12).
- To treat group members with love, patience, kindness, and gentleness (2 Timothy 2:24-25; Galatians 5:22-23; Colossians 3:12-17).

Followers

- To honor and respect authority (1 Peter 2:13-17; 1 Timothy 5:17)
- To imitate Christlike leaders (Hebrews 11 and 12:1-3)
- To do what's right; not just hear about it (James 1:22-25)

Group Case Studies

Motormouth Matt

Liz is dreading her student-led Bible study tonight. She knows that as soon as she begins to encourage discussion, Matt will take over. Matt's nickname is "Motormouth," and when he starts talking, no one else ever gets a chance. What should Liz do to deal with this situation as a student leader?

Group Gossip

Michael wonders what to do with the juicy morsel of gossip he heard about Jill, the girl that dropped out of his student-led Bible study two weeks ago. More than one person in his group has brought it to his attention during the days before the Bible study. What should he do with the information, and should he talk to the group about it?

Doug's Dilemma

Doug vowed it would never happen again. When Sara blindsided him with that "trick" question during last week's study, he was so embarrassed that he excused the group early. What should he do this week if she asks him another tough question he can't answer?

Shy Steve

Jennifer feels so sorry for Steve. He never said a word during the first six sessions of their student-led group. What should she do to draw him out?

Basic Training

Topic: Growing from failure

Supplies: You'll need photocopies of "The Seven R's of Healthy Failure" handout (p. 99), newsprint, a marker, and tape.

Preparation: Make one photocopy of "The Seven R's of Healthy Failure" hand-out (p. 99) for each person. On a piece of newsprint, write, "I really messed up when…" and tape the newsprint to a wall.

Understanding the Basics

Have students form pairs. Have partners face each other and put their hands on each other's shoulders. Instruct pairs to push their partners across the room when you give the signal. Give the signal, and have students spend a few minutes trying to push each other. Then ask:
- **How was this experience like failure in real life?**
- **What's the difference between making a mistake and failing?**
- **When have you felt "pushed around" by failure?**

Say: **Failure can be your friend or your enemy, depending on how you respond to the crisis that failure brings. Today we're going to talk about how to make failure our friend.**

Have kids form trios. Refer kids to the newsprint sign you taped to a wall earlier. Encourage students to talk in their trios about failure they've experienced.

When groups have had time to share, gather groups together, and ask volunteers to share some of their failures. Ask:
- **How did you feel when you knew you had failed?**
- **How did others respond to your failure?**
- **How do you think God reacted?**

Applying the Skill

Say: **When we're leading, failure can come in a variety of ways and situations. It's important to remember that the secret of making failure a good thing is how we handle ourselves and the situation. If we learn how to deal with failure while we're in the middle of it, we've found a great treasure.**

Have kids form groups of four. Give each person a copy of "The Seven R's of Healthy Failure" handout. Ask students to read the handout; then instruct each group to come up with a short role-play (thirty to sixty seconds) that involves failure. When groups have their ideas, say: **Remember—the secret to making it through failure is how we handle ourselves in the middle of it. As other**

groups perform their role plays, if you think of a great way to handle the failure, yell "Freeze!" and offer your idea.

Allow groups to present their situations. Encourage students to use their handouts as guides for handling failure. When someone yells "Freeze!" encourage students to voice their opinions and share their ideas.

When the role-plays are finished, say: **It's important to remember that as student leaders, people are watching you. People are looking at you to see how you handle yourself in difficult situations. Let's talk about our group now.**

Putting It Into Practice

Ask:
- **When have we experienced failure as a group?**
- **What do you wish you had done differently in these situations?**
- **How could the handout help us handle these situations?**

Have kids form pairs. Ask pairs to reread their handouts and spend a few minutes discussing their most difficult struggles in dealing with failure. Also ask pairs to talk about the "R's" on the handouts that they have the most difficulty dealing with. For example, a student might have difficulty resisting Satan's attempts to use the failure against him or her. Encourage students to pray with each other.

When students are finished praying, encourage them to take their handouts home and review them regularly.

The Seven R's
of Healthy Failure

Refuse to let others make your failure a huge issue.

Regroup by thinking through the failure, searching for what happened.

Resist Satan's attempts to use the failure against you.

Rely on God to heal you and help you recover.

Recognize that there's growth potential in failure.

Respond by making a plan to pick up the pieces from this mistake.

Rejoice that God is teaching you something new.

Basic Training

Topic: Conflict resolution

Supplies: You'll need photocopies of the "Ten Steps to a Good, Clean Fight" handout (p. 102) and a Bible.

Preparation: Make one photocopy of the "Ten Steps to a Good, Clean Fight" handout (p. 102) for each person. Ask two of your students to stage an argument at the beginning of the meeting. Encourage them to allow the argument to become verbally heated but to avoid physical contact and profanity. Tell the students to begin the argument after everyone sits down and you say, "It's time to get started." If your actors aren't sure what to fight about, have one of them make fun of the other's clothes. Instruct the other actor to overreact to the insult.

Understanding the Basics

Have kids sit down. Say: **It's time to get started.** Ramble on about your day or something else as your actors begin to argue. Allow the conflict to continue until all the attention is on your actors. Have the students stop the argument after a couple minutes.

Ask:
- **What was your initial reaction when** (names of students) **were fighting?**
- **What emotions did you experience during the argument?**
- **How would you have reacted if you were** (name of one of the actors)? **if you were** (name of the other actor)?
- **Did you want to get involved in their argument? Why or why not?**

Say: **Before this meeting, I asked these students to pretend to get into a fight. Thank you, by the way, for the excellent performance. I'm sorry if any of you felt uncomfortable during the argument, but I wanted to show you that conflict can be a very difficult and uncomfortable thing to deal with.**

Have students form groups of three to discuss these questions:
- **Have you witnessed much conflict in your area of leadership? Elaborate.**
- **Have you been *in* any conflicts as a leader? Explain.**
- **What caused most of the conflicts you've witnessed or been involved in?**

Applying the Skill

Say: **Conflict isn't necessarily a bad thing. You're going to have differences of opinion and even disagreements with the people you work with and serve. Different people have different backgrounds and different experiences. Conflict will sometimes arise out of those differences. Conflict can** also come from a misunderstanding, a hasty judgment, or a different idea of what should be done. Regardless of how conflict comes about, the way it's dealt with will shape your relationships and your effectiveness as a leader.

Ask:

● **How do you deal with conflict at home? with your friends? with the people you serve?**

● **How do you deal with conflict when two or more of the people you serve are disagreeing or fighting?**

● **What are some effective ways to handle conflict? ineffective ways?**

Give each person a copy of the "A Good, Clean Fight" handout. Ask:

● **Which of the principles on this handout did our actors fail to follow?**

● **How could the conflict have been handled more appropriately?**

Ask your actors to stand up. Have your students help the actors talk through the conflict according to the principles on their handouts.

Ask:

● **Do you think these principles are really practical? Why or why not?**

● **Can you think of other principles that should be added to the handout?**

Putting It Into Practice

Have a volunteer read Ephesians 4:26 aloud. Say: **Imagine that the fight I had staged at the beginning of this meeting was real.** Ask:

● **What do you think would happen to the actors' relationship if they never talked about what happened?**

● **How would their unresolved conflict affect the dynamics of this group?**

● **How could their unresolved conflict affect their relationships with God?**

● **Why did Paul say, "Do not let the sun go down while you are still angry?"**

Say: **Notice that Paul never said that we should never get angry. He just said we need to deal with our anger. Bitterness, unforgiveness, and unresolved conflict destroy relationships and inhibit effective ministry. Challenge the people you lead to deal with conflict. Share your handout with them, and show them how to have good, clean fights so the ministry you're involved in can stay healthy and the people you serve can continue to grow.**

Have students spend a few minutes in silent prayer. Challenge them to ask God to reveal unresolved conflict in their lives that must be dealt with. Encourage students to ask God for strength to face and deal with the issues.

Encourage students to keep their handouts for future reference.

Handout
Ten Steps to a Good, Clean Fight

1. Approach the person in humility. Keep in mind that your primary goal is to *work through the conflict*—you aren't attempting to "win" or to be right.

2. Make the conversation as private as possible. When you need to confront someone, don't do it in a way that will embarrass the person or give others an opportunity to take sides.

3. Use "I feel...because..." statements. Accusations and blame are counterproductive. Be true to your own feelings, but don't go on the offensive. For example, instead of saying, "You're acting like a child. How could you be so insensitive?" say, "*I felt* angry and embarrassed when you laughed at the story I shared *because* I was expressing some very personal feelings."

4. Avoid universal words and personal attacks. It's not fair to use the words *always* and *never* when you're addressing someone's behavior. Universal words usually make people defensive. Make it clear that you aren't judging or attacking the person, you just want to work through the feelings and effects of the behavior.

5. Stick to the point. Bringing up past mistakes and disagreements makes it difficult to work through the current issue.

6. Actively listen. Give the person an opportunity to share his or her feelings. Concentrate on what the person is saying instead of thinking about your response.

7. Extend or seek forgiveness. If you've intentionally or unintentionally hurt someone, apologize. Forgive the other person—even if he or she doesn't apologize to you.

8. Stick to the rules. The person you're having a conflict with may have poor conflict-resolution skills. Even if the person attacks or offends you, model effective conflict-resolution skills to him or her. Do everything in your power to live at peace with the person. Realize that some people may have serious personal issues that are misdirected toward you.

9. Normalize. Conflict is awkward and emotionally charged. Once you work through the conflict, help the person see that everything is OK with your relationship by telling a joke, praying with the person, making conversation, or asking the person to spend time with you.

10. Pray. If you don't feel the conflict has been resolved, ask God to intervene. If the conflict has been resolved, ask God to protect you and the person from bitterness and lies about your relationship.

Basic Training

Topic: Listening

Supplies: You'll need pens or pencils and photocopies of the "Ground Rules for Active Listening" handout (p. 105).

Preparation: Make one photocopy of the "Active Listening" handout (p. 105) for each student. Choose a slightly controversial social or church topic for the discussion in "Putting It Into Practice."

Understanding the Basics

Say: **In this session we're going to focus on listening skills—the most important of all communication skills. Listening is the best way to learn. And people love being listened to. But listening is hard work. It's a learned skill.**

Ask: **How do you usually respond to people when they talk to you about problems they're having?**

Say: **When we listen, most of us are eager to answer or comment, and we're often preparing our responses while the other people are talking. Today we're going to practice "empathic responding" or "active listening."**

Give each person a copy of the "Ground Rules for Active Listening" handout. Say: **Let's look at the ground rules for listeners.** Read through the ground rules on the handout together, and answer students' questions as necessary. Then say: **In the exercise we're about to do, your partner is going to share something personal with you, and it's important to keep that information confidential.**

Applying the Skill

Have kids form pairs, and give each student a pen or pencil. Instruct each person to think of a problem or conflict to share with his or her partner and then write about it in the space provided at the bottom of the handout. Then have pairs decide who will be the speaker first and who will be the listener.

Have students sit across from their partners. Say: **Each person will take a turn as the speaker for three minutes then as the listener for the next three minutes. Speakers, you may refer to your notes about the problem as needed, and listeners, you can glance at the ground rules as needed. Listeners, try to follow those ground rules, practicing active listening.** When everyone's ready, tell kids to begin. After two minutes, have kids switch roles.

When the exercise is finished, have each pair find another pair to form a foursome. Have groups discuss these questions:

● **Was it difficult to be the listener? Explain.**

● **How were you tempted to break the ground rules as the listener?**

● **How was this listening experience different from how you normally listen to someone?**

● **When you spoke, what was it like to have someone listen well?**

● **As you talked, did you come to a better understanding of your own problem or conflict? Did you solve your problem? If so, how?**

Say: **When you practice active listening, it often helps the speaker solve his or her own problem, or at least think of possible solutions or compromises. Let's talk about how we can put this skill of active listening into practice.**

Putting It Into Practice

Ask the entire group:

● **What are some situations in which you can employ active listening?**

● **How do you think active listening can improve your leadership skills?**

Say: **Leaders should be constantly learning, and listening is the best way to learn. Asking questions and listening lead to a better understanding of how to deal with problems and with different kinds of people. By active listening, you can nurture your group members into sharing their thoughts and ideas and feeling like part of a cohesive team. Let's try a short discussion exercise to practice more active listening.**

If you have more than ten people, have kids form two or three groups for this exercise. Name a topic for students to discuss for about five minutes. It should be a slightly controversial issue that your church or group is actually facing. Encourage teenagers to be critical thinkers when they express opinions, yet to be respectful, warm, open, and active listeners when they respond to others' opinions. Explain that everyone should be involved, taking turns to give their opinions and respond to others' comments. If you have more than one group, wander among the groups and listen, reminding kids of active listening skills and keeping them on track if necessary. After five minutes, ask:

● **What was the overall tone of this discussion?**

● **How did the group make you feel comfortable or uncomfortable when you expressed an opinion?**

● **Do you feel as if you listened to others in a different way than you used to? Explain.**

● **How might employing these techniques help our youth group?**

Congratulate teenagers on learning and applying active-listening skills. Encourage kids to take their handouts home, study the ground rules, and practice active listening with their families and friends.

Handout
Ground Rules for
Active Listening

1. Give your full attention to the speaker, make eye contact, and smile.

2. Listen to gain a clear understanding of what is being said.

3. Listen for feelings being expressed.

4. Repeat back the emotions you think that person is feeling to communicate, "I hear what you're feeling."

5. Empathize with the speaker. Your comments should communicate: "I'm listening closely to you, and this is what I hear you saying."

6. Temporarily suspend your own feelings, thoughts, and evaluations. Avoid the instinct to jump into the conversation with comments about your experience or judgments about the situation.

7. If you do ask a question, it should clarify the situation and should start with "how," "why," "what," or "where."

8. Summarize the key points you hear the speaker saying.

9. Have patience. Allow time for silence, and don't interrupt.

10. Don't destroy trust by repeating what you hear to others.

Role-Play Instructions

Identify a problem or a conflict to share with your partner when you are the speaker. It might be a problem you have with a friend or acquaintance, with school, on the job, or at home with parents or family members. Identify possible reasons for the situation and how the problem makes you feel.

Basic Training

Topic: Accountability

Supplies: You'll need photocopies of the "Relationships of Accountability" handout (pp. 108-109), photocopies of the "Accountability Commitment" handout (p. 110), index cards, pens or pencils, and a Bible.

Preparation: Make one photocopy of the "Relationships of Accountability" handout (pp. 108-109) and one photocopy of the "Accountability Commitment" handout (p. 110) for each person.

Understanding the Basics

Give each student an index card and a pen or pencil. Say: **Divide your index card into three sections. Now think about the most horrible thing you've ever done. Write down a symbol that represents that action on one section of your index card. The symbol only needs to make sense to you. On the second section of the card, write down a symbol that represents a sin you committed since the last time we met. On the third section of the card, write down a symbol that represents a sin you've committed today.**

Have everyone stand up. Then ask:

● **How would you feel if I told you we were going to take turns explaining our symbols to the entire group?**

Say: **I'm not going to ask you to share any of the symbols you've written down.**

Ask:

● **Why wouldn't you want to explain your symbols to this group?**

● **Can you think of any reason someone might want to explain his or her symbols?**

● **Why is it difficult to tell others about our mistakes and sins?**

Read James 5:16 aloud. Then say: **Every person in this group needs accountability. Confessing our sins to others and asking others for help strengthens our faith and encourages us in our relationship with God. But being truly accountable is difficult. We are naturally concerned about our own image and our own safety. Fortunately, God has provided a way for us to be accountable without having to confess our secret sins in front of the entire leadership team.**

Applying the Skill

Have students form groups of four to discuss these questions:

- **Why is it important to be accountable to others?**
- **When was there a time you were helped, challenged, or corrected by a friend?**
- **What would have happened if that friend wouldn't have been there?**

Give each person a copy of the "Relationships of Accountability" handout, and have groups of four break off into pairs. Say: **In a little while, I'm going to have you think about who you'd like to keep you accountable for the difficult issues you face. But first I'd like you to get an idea of what an accountability relationship looks like. Read your handout to learn about relationships of accountability. Then tell your partner about one area in your life you'd like him or her to pray for and to keep you accountable for until the next time we meet. It's OK if this is a surface issue. For example, you could ask your partner to keep you accountable regarding your temper, your study habits, or your attitude. Pray for each other, and remember to ask your partner how things are going next time we meet.**

When students finish, ask: **What about that exercise was difficult?**

Putting It Into Practice

Say: **One of the benefits of accountability is that it can help protect you from the damaging effects of sin. The prayers of others and the realization that we have to answer to real people can give us the strength to avoid sin. But for the relationship to work, you have to be honest, and you have to trust the person. So I'd like you to think carefully right now about who you want to have a relationship of accountability with. Most likely, it will be someone you already have a relationship with, like a friend, a parent, or a leader in the church.**

While students are thinking, give each teenager an "Accountability Commitment" handout. Say: **Decide who you will ask to help keep you accountable. You can use the accountability commitment I've given you to help you get started or simply talk with the person. As you begin your relationship of accountability, consider discussing the "Relationships of Accountability" handout with your partner.**

Relationships of Accountability

How to Be Accountable to Someone

Find someone you trust. If your best friend has accidentally leaked your secrets, your best friend probably isn't the person you should be accountable to. If you don't want to ask a friend, consider asking your pastor to hold you accountable.

Find someone who is the same gender. Accountable relationships sometimes require you to express very intimate thoughts and feelings. Someone of the opposite sex may not know how to interpret some of your feelings.

Be completely honest. Don't change the facts to make yourself look good, and don't withhold important information. Remember that the relationship is for your personal growth.

Focus on a few areas. Don't feel that you have to confess every sin you've committed since your last meeting. Your relationship of accountability isn't designed to take place of your relationship with God. It's designed to help you change patterns of behavior. Focus on the key areas in your life that God is calling you to change.

Meet regularly. Whether you decide to meet once a week or once a month, set aside a regular time to meet with your accountability partner.

Expect your partner to keep you accountable. Encourage your partner to ask the tough questions, to challenge you to grow, and to pray for you between meeting times.

How to Keep Someone Accountable

Be empathetic. Show genuine concern for the person you're keeping accountable. Don't judge or attack the person. Instead, remind him or her of God's mercy and forgiveness.

Be firm. Show compassion, but don't say something is OK if it isn't. Help your partner see the truth, and don't help him or her make excuses.

Be patient. You may grow tired of hearing about the same sin again and again. But don't lose hope. Consistently pray for your partner, and ask God to give you compassion and understanding.

Be trustworthy. Never tell anyone about the issues your partner is facing unless it is to get outside help.

Ask the tough questions. Don't condemn your partner, but make sure you help him or her face the real issues.

Remember why you're meeting. An accountability relationship isn't about making yourself appear wise or righteous. It's about helping a person grow in his or her relationship with Christ. Serve your partner, and be ready to help him or her.

Know when to get outside help. If your partner explains that he or she is planning on committing suicide, is involved in abuse, or is planning violence against another person; tell your partner you must notify someone in authority. Immediately contact your pastor or a qualified counselor. Ask your partner to come with you to talk it over. If you aren't sure whether to get outside help, ask your pastor what you should do while protecting the person's confidentiality.

Pray. It isn't your job to fix the person. It's your job to remind him or her of God's forgiveness and the standard God has called us to. Pray with your partner, asking God to bring freedom, forgiveness, and victory.

Commitment

I, _____, agree to allow _____
to keep me accountable for the issues God wants me to deal with.

I, _____, agree to keep _____
accountable for the issues God has directed him or her to deal with.

We agree to meet together _____ time(s) a month to talk and
pray about these issues. Our first meeting will be on the _____ day
of the month of _____ at _____. We
will meet regularly for _____ months then discuss whether the relationship of accountability should continue.

_____   _____
signature   signature

Basic Training

Topic: Responsibility

Supplies: You'll need photocopies of the "Responsibilities and Resources" handout (p. 113), photocopies of the "Sticky Situations" handout (p. 114), photocopies of "The Bible Says…" handout (p. 115), newsprint, a marker, tape, pens or pencils, and Bibles.

Preparation: Make one photocopy of the "Responsibilities and Resources" handout (p. 113), one photocopy of the "Sticky Situations" handout (p. 114), and one photocopy of "The Bible Says…" handout (p. 115) for each person.

Understanding the Basics

Begin by writing the word "responsibility" on a piece of newsprint taped to a wall. Ask students to define the word. As they share their thoughts, write them on the newsprint with the word.

Say: **A responsibility is a duty or obligation. In a sense, a responsibility is a course of action that we owe someone else. To have responsibility for something means that we are accountable for it. In other words, we must answer for our choices and our behavior. After all, actions always have consequences for ourselves and for people and things around us.**

Give each person a copy of the "Responsibilities and Resources" handout and a pen or pencil; then say: **On this handout, identify some specific things you're responsible for on a day-to-day basis. Think about what is expected of you in your home, school, place of work (if you have a job), and community. List them under "Everyday responsibilities" on your handout.**

After a few minutes, ask volunteers to share their answers with the rest of the class while you write their responses on a piece of newsprint. Then have someone read aloud Mark 12:28-29. Ask: **According to Jesus, what are our two main responsibilities?**

While kids respond, draw a cross on your newsprint. Write "love God" and "love other people" on the two sides of the cross (see illustration). Then say: **Loving God and loving other people aren't just a couple of lofty goals—these are the most important responsibilities we have. Write them on the two sides of the cross that's under the "Two main responsibilities" heading on your handout.**

LOVE GOD

LOVE OTHER PEOPLE

When kids have finished writing, ask:

● **Do you think it's possible to fulfill your everyday responsibilities while living up to your two main responsibilities?**

● **Can you think of times or circumstances when your two main responsibilities and your everyday responsibilities conflict?**

● **If these two sets of responsibilities seem to be conflicting, which ones do you think should take priority? Why?**

Applying the Skill

Give each person a copy of the "Sticky Situations" handout, and have kids read the stories on the handout. Then ask:

● **What seems to be the common denominator in these stories?**
● **Who was really to blame for the situations? Explain.**
● **How could these people have managed their responsibilities better?**

Putting It Into Practice

Say: **In order to handle responsibility well, people need to have good management skills.** Ask: **What are some characteristics of good management?**

Say: **Among other things, good managers know how to use the resources available to them.** Ask: **What are some resources all of us have access to?**

Have kids form pairs and exchange their "Responsibilities and Resources" handouts. Instruct partners to read each other's lists of everyday responsibilities and identify the resources they must manage well in order to meet those responsibilities. Instruct kids to make their ideas as specific as possible and to write them down under "Resources to be managed."

After a few minutes, have pairs exchange handouts again. Then ask two volunteers to read aloud Mark 8:34 and Luke 14:27. While these verses are being read, write the words "Carry your own cross" on a piece of newsprint. Ask:

● **What do you think Jesus meant when he said to carry our own crosses?**
● **Why do you think we are expected to carry crosses?**

While kids are sharing their ideas, give each person a copy of "The Bible Says..." handout. Say: **I'd like to challenge you to think of a cross as a responsibility, not just a burden. Although we may not be able to understand why we carry certain crosses, Jesus has a reason for asking us to carry them. In closing, I want you to think about what your unique, personal cross might be. Considering your particular abilities and your life circumstances, what might Jesus expect you to do? Write your response at the bottom of your handout.**

Encourage students to take their handouts with them to refer to later.

Responsibilities and Resources

Everyday responsibilities:

1.

2.

3.

4.

5.

Two main responsibilities:

Resources to be managed:

1.

2.

3.

4.

5.

Handout
Sticky Situations

Shelly had a big math test coming up the next day when her best friend called about an argument she'd had with her mother. After spending two and a half hours on the phone with her friend, Shelly was too tired to concentrate on math and went to bed. When she got a C- on the test, she was annoyed with her friend for keeping her from studying.

During the summer, Travis earned "spending money" for his first semester at college. In July his brother asked if he could borrow two hundred dollars to buy a stereo on sale, and Travis gave it to him. In August Travis dipped into his earnings to get his parents an anniversary present, and then he spent another fifty dollars on tickets to a professional basketball game just before he left for school. When October came around, Travis still hadn't heard from his brother, so he asked his parents for money to take his date to homecoming.

Keith was invited to interview with a company he hoped to work for, so he bought a sport coat, a shirt, and a tie, and he took extra care getting dressed for his appointment. On the way there, however, he saw that his gas tank was nearly empty, so he lost some time filling up at a station. To make matters worse, he encountered road construction, missed a turn, and had to drive several miles farther before he was able to turn around. His interviewer was not impressed when Keith arrived fifteen minutes late and mumbled something about the traffic.

The Bible Says...

What does the Bible say about responsibility?

- A responsibility is a duty or obligation, sometimes requiring sacrifice.

  "But the four principle gatekeepers…were entrusted with the responsibility for the rooms and the treasuries in the house of God."—1 Chronicles 9:26

  "If anyone would come after me, he must deny himself and take up his cross and follow me."—Mark 8:34b

- Responsibility leads to accountability for one's behavior.

  "So then, each of us will give an account of himself to God."—Romans 14:12

  "Give an account of your management…"—Luke 16:2b

- Responsibility requires management skills.

  "Whoever can be trusted with very little can also be trusted with much."—Luke 16:10

  "If anyone does not know how to manage his own family, how can he take care of God's church?"—1 Timothy 3:5

What is my cross?

(Remember, a cross is not a burden we bear without cause; it's a responsibility Jesus gives us to achieve a purpose.)

Basic Training

Topic: Prayer

Supplies: You'll need photocopies of the "Words of Wisdom" handout (p. 118), photocopies of the "Prayer Memo" handout (p. 119), newsprint, a marker, tape, Bibles, and pens or pencils. Small file boxes and blank index cards are optional (you may want to provide each student with some cards, glue, and a file box to start a prayer journal file). Soft music and a cassette or CD player are also optional.

Preparation: Before the session, make one photocopy of the "Words of Wisdom" handout (p. 118) and several photocopies of the "Prayer Memo" handout (p. 119) for each student. Write out the following questions on newsprint, and tape them to a wall where everyone will be able to see them:

● Is there a specific situation in your life this might apply to? Explain.

● If you applied these words in a practical way, how would your life change?

● Do these words remind you of someone you know that might need help? If so, what are some creative ways you can minister to that person?

Understanding the Basics

Say: **When you were a child, before you went to bed at night, you may have prayed the prayer, "Now I lay me down to sleep." But now that you're older, you probably have different worries. You may find that simple rote prayers aren't sufficient to meet your needs and concerns. On the other hand, you may be thinking that prayer—real prayer—is a heavy-duty procedure only for heavy-duty religious types. Sometimes, too, the idea of prayer is accompanied by heavy-duty guilt. We feel that we're not praying right or we're not praying enough.**

Let's put that guilt behind us and start praying now. Some of you can help us move away from guilt and affirm us in our faith by reading aloud Psalm 23. Following the reading of each verse, let's each offer up a silent response of thanksgiving to God.

You may want to play some soft music at this point. Have six volunteers each read aloud one verse of Psalm 23. Ask readers to pause after each verse so students can offer up silent prayers of their own. After the last verse, pause and then say "amen."

Applying the Skill

Say: **Now we're going to do some creative thinking.** Ask students to form groups of four, and give each student a "Words of Wisdom" handout.

Within each group, have each student read one card aloud. After each person reads, have the group discuss the questions you wrote out beforehand.

When groups are finished discussing, ask volunteers to share insights and ideas their groups came up with.

Then say: **As you can see, you can cut these quotations apart. Then you can glue them on cards if you want, and use them to start a prayer journal file.** (If you're providing file boxes and index cards for students, hand them out at this time.) **You can use a small file box to keep prayer cards on file. You may want to include these and other quotations to remind you of the importance of prayer. In fact, you could use these words of wisdom as section dividers, filing your prayer cards with the most appropriate quotations.**

Putting It Into Practice

Say: **Often we come to God only when we're facing huge, overwhelming problems. And maybe you see your life as one big problem! But we don't see the positive things we can thank God for. Let's see if we can come up with some positive things to thank God for, along with requests to bring to God. To do that, we'll practice filling out some prayer cards for your prayer-journal files.**

Give each student a Bible, a pen or pencil, and a "Prayer Memo" handout; then have students form pairs. Tell students to quickly read over the sample prayer card on the handout. Then have each student fill in another one of the prayer cards with a person's name or a circumstance to pray about with his or her partner. Encourage students to make the requests specific, but be sure they don't break personal confidences. And remind students to include a positive thing to thank God for.

Have partners work together to look up Bible verses that apply to their requests. After a few minutes, ask them to exchange cards and pray for each other's requests, including the thanksgiving.

As students leave, give each one several more copies of the "Prayer Memo" handout to use in their prayer-journal files.

Handout
Words of Wisdom

CARD #2

"How often we look upon God as our last and feeblest resource! We go to him because we have nowhere else to go. And then we learn that the storms of life have driven us, not upon the rocks, but into the desired haven."
—George Macdonald

CARD #4

"Be willing to lead others in prayer....You'll never know how bad some people want to pray and just can't or don't know how! So don't be embarrassed. Praying for people could change their lives—and yours!"—Becky Tirabassi

CARD #1

"Let us then approach the throne of grace with confidence, so that we may receive mercy and find grace to help us in our time of need."
—Hebrews 4:16

CARD #3

"Pray also for me, that whenever I open my mouth, words may be given me so that I will fearlessly make known the mystery of the gospel."
—Ephesians 6:19

Handout

Prayer Memo

Date:

Concern:

Thanksgiving:

My response today:

Scripture:

Outcome:

Date: February 22

Concern: Randy's not fitting in with the group. They're making fun of him behind his back.

Thanksgiving: I thank God that Randy's here and so willing to hear about Christ.

My response today: I'll talk to Mike about his attitude toward Randy.

Scripture: 1 Thessalonians 1:2 "We always thank God for all of you, mentioning you in our prayers."

Outcome: Mike didn't take it too well, but he's coming around. I can see some real changes in Randy's life.

Date:

Concern:

Thanksgiving:

My response today:

Scripture:

Outcome:

Date:

Concern:

Thanksgiving:

My response today:

Scripture:

Outcome:

Basic Training

Topic: Affirmation

Supplies: You'll need photocopies of "The Power of Affirmation" handout (p. 122), newsprint, a marker, scissors, tape, a candy bar for each person, pens or pencils, and index cards.

Preparation: Make one photocopy of "The Power of Affirmation" handout (p. 122) for each person. Write various affirming statements on newsprint, cut them apart, and tape them on one wall in your meeting room.

Understanding the Basics

As kids arrive, greet each one with a handshake or a pat on the back. Be sure you look everyone in the eye and tell each person how glad you are that he or she was able to make it to the meeting. Also hand each person a candy bar.

When everyone has arrived, ask:

● **Did you like the way I greeted you today? Why?**

● **Who can give me a clear definition of what affirmation is?**

Say: **Many of you may not completely understand what affirmation is. Let's try a simple exercise to understand it better.**

Have kids form two teams. Have each team form a single file line and stand on the opposite side of the room from the wall containing the affirmations. The teams should be standing next to each other, as in a relay race. Say: **As you can see, I've taped some pieces of paper on the wall. Each of those pieces of paper contains an affirmation. When it's your turn, you'll run down to the wall, pull an affirmation off the wall, and run back to the team. Then you must find someone the affirmation fits and place it on that person's foot. Once you've done that, you must look that person in the eyes and say the affirmation. For example, if you pick an affirmation that says, "Incredible smile," you must run over to someone, place it on his or her shoe, and say, "You have an incredible smile!" Once someone has delivered an affirmation, the next person in line may go.**

Give students a few seconds to organize their strategies, and then yell "Go!" The game continues until everyone has had a chance to affirm someone. When the game is over, ask:

● **How did it feel when you got affirmed?**

● **How did it feel trying to affirm people? Why?**

● **Did you like getting affirmed at such a quick pace? Would you have liked more time to enjoy your affirmation? Why?**

Say: **Affirmation is an important leadership skill for a number of reasons. Let's talk about why we affirm.**

Applying the Skill

Have kids form four groups, and give each person a copy of "The Power of Affirmation" handout and a pen or pencil. Say: **In your group, read the "Effects of Affirmation" list on your handout and add your own reasons why affirming someone is such a powerful idea.**

Give students a few minutes to complete their handouts. When they're finished, ask each group to share its answers. Then ask:

● **If you could pick a favorite reason from what you've heard, which one would it be? Why?**

● **How could affirmation change our group?**

Putting It Into Practice

Have students gather together as one big group. Say: **The real power behind affirmation is not how creative we are but that we do it. Many times we have great ideas and intentions but never follow through. Let's spend a few moments thinking of times when others might need affirmation.**

Give each person an index card. Ask students to write on their cards descriptions of situations they think would call for affirmation. Ask kids not to suggest how they'd go about affirming the people in the situations.

When kids are finished writing, collect the cards. Then read each situation aloud, and ask kids to brainstorm about ways to affirm the person. Direct students to the "Affirmation in Action" section of their handouts for ideas.

Say: **I'm glad you've learned basic affirmation skills today. I'm proud of you! I hope you'll be looking for times when you can affirm others. Remember to take your handouts with you for ideas.**

Close in prayer.

Handout
The Power of Affirmation

The Effects of Affirmation

1. It changes our attitude about life.
2. It tells us we aren't alone.
3. It reassures us that we're cared for.
4. It raises our level of confidence.
5. It boosts our self-esteem.
6. _____
7. _____
8. _____

Affirmation in Action

● **Puzzle Affirmations**—Find a simple puzzle and put it together. Once it's assembled, flip it over and write an encouraging note on the back—use the whole space! Then take the puzzle apart and put it back in the box. Send it to the person you're affirming.

● **Surprise Gift**—Show up at your affirmation target's home with a surprise gift.

● **Video Affirmation**—Get three of your friends together, and make a video affirmation. Film in various places you might see the person—school, work or even a friend's house. Then secretly deliver it to the person you're affirming.

● **Service**—Serve the person you're affirming! Sometimes helpful encouragement comes when a friend attempts to lighten the load. Offer to help your friend with daily chores, homework, or other things.

● **Virtual Flowers**—If the person you're affirming has an e-mail address, send that person a virtual bouquet of flowers. Do a search for "virtual flowers," find a web site, and follow the instructions.

● **Affirmation Attack**—Secretly arrange a large number of people to affirm your affirmation target throughout the day. Make sure your scheme includes significant affirmations that will happen all day.

Basic Training

Topic: Integrity

Supplies: You'll need photocopies of the "Decisions and Consequences" handout (pp. 125-126), photocopies of the "Characteristics of Principle-Centered Leaders" handout (pp. 127-128), newsprint, a marker, and pens or pencils.

Preparation: Make one photocopy of the "Decisions and Consequences" handout (pp. 125-126) and one photocopy of the "Characteristics of Principle-Centered Leaders" handout (pp. 127-128) for each student.

Understanding the Basics

Say: **Think of someone you admire or respect—an adult or teenager you know personally.** Pause. **Now think of why you admire or respect that person and of some of the qualities he or she has.** Pause. **Now tell me what some of those reasons and qualities are.**

As kids name qualities, list them on newsprint. Then ask:

- **Would you say this person you admire has integrity? Why?**
- **How would you define integrity?**

Say: **Today we're going to commit to becoming people of integrity. True leaders have integrity. Integrity means having sound moral principles, having a good reputation, being someone people can depend on, and behaving in a way that's consistent with what you say you believe.** Ask:

- **What are some other qualities of a person with integrity?**

As kids name qualities list them on another sheet of newsprint.

- **What are some ways we could become people of integrity?**

Say: **One good guideline to follow to become a person of integrity is to ask yourself, "What would Jesus do?" When you have to make a difficult decision or handle a difficult situation, ask yourself that question and pray for guidance. Having integrity doesn't mean you always make the right decision, but it means you always take responsibility for your own actions, good or bad. Let's consider some situations that might require difficult decisions that will show your true character.**

Applying the Skill

Have teenagers form groups of three or four. Give each person a copy of the "Decisions and Consequences" handout and a pen or pencil. Instruct students to read and discuss the situations with their groups and answer the questions on the handout. Each student should fill out his or her own handout.

When groups are finished, have volunteers share some of their answers. You might ask, "What would Jesus do?" for each situation.

Say: **Many of us are faced with situations like these every day—situations that test our honesty, integrity, and basic goodness. And as student leaders, it's part of your responsibility to set an example for those around you.** Ask:

- **As a person of integrity, how can you impact other people?**
- **How can that make you a better leader?**

Say: **Having integrity gives you confidence. You let the knowledge of what's right and what's wrong guide your decisions. Philippians 4:8 is a good guideline: "Whatever is true, whatever is noble, whatever is right, whatever is pure, whatever is lovely, whatever is admirable—if anything is excellent or praiseworthy—think about such things."**

Putting It Into Practice

Say: **As Christian leaders, you're often under close scrutiny. Other people expect you to be people of integrity. Hypocrisy can destroy your relationship with God and the respect you've earned from others. Hypocrisy means pretending you're something you aren't.** Ask:

- **What are some examples of ways Christians practice hypocrisy?**
- **How can you avoid hypocrisy?**

Give each person a photocopy of the "Principle-Centered Leaders" handout. Have students read their handouts and fill in the space below each statement. When kids are finished, encourage them to share their ideas for commitment to becoming principle-centered leaders.

Encourage teenagers to take their handouts home and refer to them often to remind them of their commitments and to follow through on them.

1. There's a disruptive person in your youth group. He's a clown, but he isn't very funny. He doesn't participate in activities. He always shows up and just goofs off. Some of the people in the group have talked about asking him to leave—kicking him out. You, the other student leaders, and your youth group leader have to decide what to do.

● What choices do you have in this situation?

● What are the consequences of those choices?

● What would you choose to do?

2. Your youth group has been working extremely hard on a fund-raiser for a missions project. Many needy people will benefit from your group's efforts. Several of you have gone to the store to buy supplies for your fund-raiser, and the cost is pretty high—over $300. When the clerk rings up your sale, she makes a mistake and tells you your total is $130. You tell her that can't be right, but she insists that it is. You think, "Wow, that's more money that can be spent on the missions project," but you know it isn't right to pay less than you owe.

● What choices do you have in this situation?

● What are the consequences of those choices?

● What would you choose to do?

3. A member of your youth group likes to tell others she's a Christian, and she often shares her faith with friends and strangers. She's always the first to volunteer for projects at church and the first to answer discussion questions. Yesterday at school you overheard her in the hall, spreading some nasty gossip about another member of your youth group, who happens to be your friend. Later, you confronted her about her actions, and she lied, denying the incident.

● What choices do you have in this situation?

- What are the consequences of those choices?

- What would you choose to do?

4. A person at school you don't know very well asked if you'd like to do something Friday night—bowling or a movie. You agreed to go, but then you had second thoughts. The person is kind of a nerd, and you were afraid your regular group of friends might make fun of you. Now it's Friday evening, and you called at the last minute and told the person you were sick. You felt bad about it and said, "Let's do something next week," but you really have no intention of doing that. You've gone out with your friends, and you've run into the person at a restaurant. The person is walking toward you, probably wanting an explanation.

- What choices do you have in this situation?

- What are the consequences of those choices?

- What would you choose to do?

5. One of your non-Christian friends is throwing a party. Even though you suspected there would be alcohol at the party, you decided to go so you could get to know your friend better and perhaps even be an influence for positive behavior. Now that you're at the party, you're actually having fun. Other people have been really friendly, and some of the people who never talk to you at school are treating you like one of them. You've been walking around the room with a glass of lemon-lime soda. Suddenly another person walks up and says loudly, "Wow! You're drinking hard liquor? I didn't know you drank!"

- What choices do you have in this situation?

- What are the consequences of those choices?

- What would you choose to do?